Llewellyn's
Herbal Almanac
2012

Editor: Sharon Leah

Cover Design: Kevin R. Brown

Cover Images: Mint: iStockphoto.com, Evgeniy Ivanov; Vanilla Flower and Mint Herb: iStockphoto.com, Eleonora Kolotseva; Tea Cup with Rose Hits: iStockphoto.com, Eleonora Ivanova; Basil, Parsley, Cilantro: iStockphoto.com, Wendy Miranda; Italian Parsley in Flower Pot, French Tarragon in Flower Pot, and Sweet Marjoram Herb Icon: iStockphoto.com, Joan Loitz; Sunflower: iStockphoto.com, Alex van de Hoef

Interior Art: © Fiona King, excluding illustrations on pages 2–4, which are © Mary Azarian

You can order annuals and books from *New Worlds*, Llewellyn's catalog. To request a free copy, call toll free: 1-877-NEW WRLD, or visit our website at http://www.llewellyn.com.

ISBN 978-0-7387-1205-5
Llewellyn Worldwide Ltd.
2143 Wooddale Drive
Woodbury, MN 55125-2989

Table of Contents

Growing and Gathering Herbs

Culinary Herbs

Herbs for Health and Beauty

Herb Crafts

Herb History, Myth, and Lore

Moon Signs, Phases, and Tables

Introduction to Llewellyn's
Herbal Almanac

The herbal landscape is an ever-evolving one. The slow warming of our planet has seen temperate climates creeping toward the poles, while consumer trends prompt more immediate changes. But through it all, homegrown herbs still make a lasting impact. *Llewellyn's 2012 Herbal Almanac* takes a look at the year-round effects of herbs, re-examining the research on uses of herbs as medicine, as culinary spices, as cosmetics, and more. This year we once again tap into practical, historical, and just plain enjoyable aspects of herbal knowledge—using herbs to help people manage personal energy flow, combat pesky insects, craft with herbs, plant and care for herb gardens, make infusions, tinctures, and teas; and, of course, trying out fabulous new recipes. And we bring to these pages some of the most innovative and original thinkers and writers on herbs.

Growing, preparing, and using herbs allows us to focus on the old ways—when men and women around the world knew and understood the power of herbs. Taking a step back to a simpler time is important today as the pace of everyday life quickens and demands more and more of our energy—leaving precious little room for beauty, good food, health, love, and friendship. This state of affairs is perhaps not terribly surprising considering so many of us are out of touch with the beauty, spirituality, and health-giving properties of the natural world. Many of us spend too much of our lives rushing about in a technological bubble. We forget to focus on the parts of life that can bring us back into balance and harmony.

Though it's getting more difficult, you can still find ways to escape the rat race once in a while. People are still striving to make us all more aware of the uplifting, beautiful ways that herbs can affect our lives. In the 2012 edition of the *Herbal Almanac*, the authors pay tribute to the ideals of beauty and balance in relation to the health-giving and beautifying properties of herbs. Whether it comes in the form of energy-opening herbs, crafting your own bug repellents, or a new favorite recipe, herbs can clearly make a positive impact in your life.

Herbs are the perfect complement to the power of the mind, an ancient tool whose time has come back around to help us restore balance in our lives. More and more people are using herbs, growing and gathering them, and studying them for their enlivening and healing properties. We, the editor and authors of this volume, encourage the treatment of the whole organism—of the person and of the planet—with herbal goodness.

Growing
and
Gathering
Herbs

Urban Herb Gardening Tips

❧ by JD Hortwort ❧

Most herbs are tolerant of harsh growing conditions—even those found in our urban centers, which are man-made heat wells. With a little direction and some perseverance, urban gardeners can grow plenty of herbs for the kitchen, bath, or cupboard.

It is a lucky urban gardener, indeed, who has access to a plot of land for gardening. Some cities provide access to community garden land.[1] But if a little piece of land isn't available, the urban gardener often turns to container gardening. Fortunately, gardening in containers allows the grower to maximize limited space.

1. Check with your local Cooperative Extension or city recreation department to see what is available in your area.

Most culinary herbs will fill out a large pot, and any herb that trails across the ground can be encouraged to run up a trellis.

If you want to plant herbs and you have limited space, the first thing to do is survey what you have available and choose the most appropriate growing space. Even plants that are grown in containers will need adequate light. The best growing location is a southern exposure that gets sun throughout the day. A western exposure, where the sun hits the location from midday onward, is next best. Finally, an eastern exposure that sees sunlight from early morning until around noon will work well for many herb plants. While most herb plants need at least four hours of direct sunlight, it's possible to grow a selection of herbs that will survive in the shade. Your choices will be limited, though. Northern exposures that receive no sunlight will be very challenging!

Tips on Containers, Soil, and Planting

Let's work from the assumption that light will not be a problem, even if the available space is only a windowsill. The next step is to develop the "land." You need pots that are at least 12 inches deep to accommodate plant roots. Garden centers usually carry a variety of sizes, and the 10- to 15-gallon plastic pots are excellent. Don't forget those pickle buckets that restaurants go through by the dozens. Both of these types of containers are big enough to grow a variety of herbs, but they are not too big to move around once they are filled. As an added benefit, they tend to be free! If you do use pickle buckets, punch some holes in the bottom of the buckets before filling them with potting soil.

Of course, pretty containers can be purchased from a department store or garden center. Plastic pots are ideal, though, because they are durable and lightweight. Terra cotta pots are very attractive, but they can be heavy, and they must be protected from cold weather, as they are likely to break from freezing and thawing. The new foam pots that have become available more recently are, like plastic pots, durable and lightweight. Some are so well made that it's hard to tell them from a terra cotta pot—until you try to pick one up!

As a rule, it's hard to go wrong with a general-purpose potting soil. It will support most annual herbs, like basil, parsley, sage, coriander, and Clary sage. Ironically, if you are growing culinary herbs, you can save yourself some money by purchasing plain soil, because culinary herbs don't need a lot of fertilizer. Feeding them with a general-purpose fertilizer at the time of planting and then once more midway through the growing season is enough.[2] Fertilizing more often will result in lush growth that has little flavor. A great thing about herbs is that they are tough little fighters, and "roughing it" helps them to develop the right amount of essential oils.

This is especially true of the herbs such as lavender, rosemary, thyme, oregano, and marjoram that originated in the Mediterranean area. In this case, purchasing a soil mixed for succulents, which is formulated to drain well, would be a good idea. If you can't find this type of soil, it's easy to make. Just mix one part coarse builder's sand with two parts general purpose potting soil and you're all set!

Begin the setup of your containers by adding a one-inch layer of pebbles to the bottom of the pot. This will allow the

2. A general-purpose fertilizer has equal amounts of nitrogen, phosphorous, and potassium.

container to drain and help prevent the soil from pouring out of the bottom of the pot. If you have access to old broken terra cotta pots, the shards make excellent material for covering the holes at the bottom of a container without totally blocking them.

Fill the containers up to two-thirds full with soil if you are using sets or plants from a garden center. If you plan to use a granular fertilizer, read the package directions and add the recommended amount of fertilizer now. Be sure to mix the fertilizer and soil together to avoid burning the root ball of your plants. If you use a liquid fertilizer, wait until planting is finished before adding fertilizer.

A 10-gallon container will hold up to three 15- to 18-inch tall plants. A 15-gallon pot can handle up to five such sets. A single plant that gets bigger, like rosemary, will quickly fill a 10-gallon container in two growing seasons. Check the plant tags that come with most nursery plants. They usually tell how big a plant will be at maturity.

When you plant each herb set in the container, the top of the root ball should come to roughly two inches below the rim of the container. If you don't have enough soil, add more now. Herbs that are set too low in the container will likely die from crown rot. Those that are set too high will dry out quickly and probably die from stress.

As you add plants, surround them with soil. Once all plants are in the pot, add more soil, firming as you go. Now, water the plants thoroughly to settle out any air pockets in the mixture.

If you are planting seeds, fill the pot to within two inches from the top of the pot. Read the directions on the back of the seed packet carefully. Some seeds are so "fine" they need to be distributed on top of the soil. Some need to be barely covered with soil, and others can be buried one or two inches deep. The packet should also tell you when to expect your seeds to sprout.

Keeping soil moisture consistent is critical for seedlings. Watch tender, little plants carefully and if necessary, move the container out of the hot afternoon sunlight until the new plants develop a sufficient root system.

Once the plants are established, adding a layer of mulch will help control the moisture content of the soil. Mulch will also keep your herbs clean by prohibiting the soil from splashing up on the plants during rains or when you water.

As you plan your container garden, give some thought to the layout. You don't have to segregate your plants. In fact, mixing compatible herbs is a great way to add visual interest. Just be sure to mix those plants that have similar growing requirements. Thyme, oregano, garlic, chives, marjoram, artemisia, and pennyroyal need good drainage to grow well. They also appreciate that lean soil mixture of potting soil and sand mentioned earlier.

Anise, hyssops, calendulas, lemon balm, borage, santolina, sage, and tarragon are full plants that like average potting soil. Several of these plants come in a variety of colorful foliage that will give you plenty of design options as well as useful harvests for cooking or crafts.

Don't forget to look up as you garden. A trellis in the back of a large pot will give passionflower vine and sweet peas something to grow on, or a place to support tall herbs such as cat mint, dill, and tansy. Some herbs work well in hanging baskets. Scented geraniums are naturals for hanging containers, as are nasturtiums.

Mixing annual and perennial herbs, especially in the first season, is a good way to adjust for robust plants later. For example, you can mix perennial lavender and annual calendulas in a 10-gallon pot the first year. But by the second year, the lavender will probably prefer to be left alone in its pot.

Container gardening is an adventure in learning. While books and Internet sources can get you started, nothing beats getting your hands in the soil and finding out what works for you. A golden rule in gardening is "You've got to grow it to know it." Find out for yourself if basil planted with thyme works for you. Will you be a mint lover? How many times will you have to plant oregano to get it to flourish for you?

Push your boundaries. Test your limits. Create your own little green spot wherever you live and thumb your nose at that concrete jungle that surrounds you.

Herbal Honey Harvests

⁂ by Suzanne Ress ⁂

Bees love nearly every flowering herb plant. During the summer and early autumn months, blooming herb gardens will attract honey bees from the nearest beekeeper's apiary, as well as wild bees, bumble bees, and butterflies. All of these valuable insects contribute to the pollination of herb plants, making the plants' seeds viable for the following year. Of all pollinating insects, though, honey bees are our most precious friends.

While most pollinating insects might flit from a lavender flower to a sage blossom to a purple coneflower, a honey bee will fly from one flower to another of the same species of plant—for example, lavender—until her honey sacs are filled with nectar. This means that the pollen she inadvertently picks up on her tiny feet while sipping the flower's nectar will be carried to the next flower of that same plant or type of plant. This is very efficient pollination, and it makes fruit (seed) possible from all of the flowers of that plant.

A honey bee sticks with one species of plant at a time because, unlike other pollinating insects, she uses the flowers' nectar to make honey. Each species of plant flower produces nectar with different sugar and water contents, and for the transformation of nectar into honey it is essential to start with nectars that have the same amounts of sugar and water. The honey bee knows this, so she keeps each type of flower nectar separate from the others until the nectar has been made into honey in the comb.

Flower nectar contains 20 to 60 percent sucrose and the rest is water. Honey, on the other hand, usually contains 40 to 50 percent fructose, and 25 to 50 percent dextrose, only trace amounts of sucrose, and less than 20 percent water. How do honey bees transform sucrose into fructose and dextrose, what is the difference between these sugars, and how do the bees get rid of the excess water from the nectar?

The human body cannot use complex sugar, so the digestive tract uses enzymes and fermentation to break down sucrose (sugar) into the simple sugars fructose and dextrose. The simple sugar dextrose enters the blood and fuels muscles. The other simple sugar, fructose, is stored as glycogen in the liver. When the body needs it, the stored glycogen is transformed into dextrose. Because the sugars in honey are simple sugars, they are easier for us to digest than complex (cane) sugar, and much of the energy from honey can be used as instant fuel.

Basically, honey is sugar water that has been pre-digested, brought to the perfect water-to-sugar ratio to prevent spoilage, and then sealed under wax caps—all by thousands of honey bees.

As soon as a bee takes nectar from a flower into her honey sac, the process of inversion begins to change the sucrose into fructose and dextrose. A field (pollinator) honey bee makes between ten and thirty nectar-collecting trips out of the hive in a day, returning to the hive only when her honey sac is full. To fill her honey sac, she must visit anywhere between 50 and 1,000 flowers, depending on the size of the flower, how much nectar it contains, and how easily her proboscis can reach that nectar.

When her honey sac is filled and she returns to the hive, the field bee is met near the entrance to the hive by several house bees. She gives part of her load of nectar to some of these bees, and then enters into the hive. She soon encounters another house bee to whom she gives the rest of her honey load, then she hurries to the comb area where food is kept (the "kitchen" area in the hive) for a quick snack of bee bread (made of pollen), cleans herself up a bit and takes off again to the field for her next collecting trip.

In the meantime, the house bee makes her way into a not-too-crowded place in the hive and finds an empty or partially-filled cell (storage place) in the wax comb. She will remain there for ten to twenty minutes, manipulating the inverted flower nectar with her mouth parts to remove some of its water content. She then deposits the honey nectar into the cell where, over the course of about three days, it will evaporate further until it has reached a sugar (fructose/dextrose) concentration of 80 percent. The bees know that with 20 percent or less water, honey cannot ferment or spoil. At this point, the house bee will seal the cell of finished honey with a wax cap.

In a strong healthy hive, there are about 30,000 field bees. Depending on weather conditions, nectar flow, and other factors, a single bee colony can gather up to five pounds of honey per day. Keep in mind, however, that it takes 300 bees working full time to collect enough nectar during the "honey flow" to make a single pound of honey.

The "honey flow" is when certain trees (like the chestnut), or vast carpets of wild thyme, or fields full of lavender, or orange or almond tree orchards, are in bloom. During the honey flow, bees work very hard to gather nectar. A honey flow only lasts as long as the flowers of the particular plant or tree are in bloom—no longer than two or three weeks, and usually less.

Herbal honeys are honeys produced naturally by bees using primarily, or almost exclusively, the nectar from a single type of flowering herb. Do not confuse herb-infused honey with natural herbal honey! Herb-infused honeys, while delicious in their own right, are concocted by humans, who put freshly cut herbs or spices into a mild flavored light honey, such as clover honey.

In order for honey to be considered monofloral herbal honey, as opposed to being a general wildflower or forest flower honey, most or all of the nectar brought into the hive during the honey flow must come from a single plant source. How do we know what plant a colony's honey comes from?

In order to make monofloral honey from herbs, bees must have access to a huge quantity of the same type of herbal flowers. For example, to produce one pound of wild-thyme honey requires the nectar from about 4.5 million tiny wild thyme flowers. This means, basically, acres and acres of wild thyme must be in bloom. Some locations in Greece or Sicily, and even parts of rural New England, have enough wild thyme blooming naturally for this herbal honey to be made.

Lavender flowers grown in southern France for the perfume industry must be pollinated by honey bees that then produce lavender honey.

I live on a small farm in northern Italy. Our land is surrounded by many acres of chestnut and black locust (acacia) forest. Since I am a stationary beekeeper, as opposed to being an itinerant one, my bee colonies only experience two main honey flows each summer. First, the black locust trees bloom in late May, and then the chestnut trees bloom in late June. Once the chestnut trees have stopped blooming and shed their flowers, by around July 10, the bees must depend on the floral nectar from my large and ever expanding herb gardens, and I am ever so happy to help them in this small and pleasant way.

One of the bees' favorite herbal flowers is lavender. When my plot full of these plants first comes into bloom, it acts as a honey bee magnet. Later, when the flowers start to fade a little, large numbers of bumble bees and butterflies of all kinds and colors appear, like a great shimmering fairy cloud above it.

Bees love my thyme plants, of course, and they also crowd around the marjoram and oregano when it blooms. Sage is a popular herbal bee plant, as are savory, purple coneflower, mint, beebalm, lemon verbena, lemon balm, horehound, wild fennel, borage, coriander, dill, parsley, basil, chamomile, rue, and just about any other aromatic blooming herb plant. The exceptions are artemisia wormwood, tarragon, mugwort, and southernwood, and feverfew.

Bees can make herbal honey from nearly any herb plant if there is enough of it in bloom at the same time! Some of the most common herbal honeys are:

Bell heather honey (*Erica cinerea*) is made from heather that grows in the Scottish Highlands. This honey is very dark reddish-brown in color and has a characteristic strong flavor.

Coriander honey (*Coriandrum sativum*) can be made anywhere there is enough coriander in bloom! It is a pale golden crystallized honey, with a medium sweet, slightly spicy taste.

Dandelion honey (*Taraxacum officinale*) is a cream-colored or light-amber honey that has a strong and pungent, although pleasing, flavor. Like golden rod, dandelions are essential to bees, for they bloom when nothing else does, and produce a rich source of pollen and nectar.

Goldenrod honey (*Solidago virgaurea*) is a deep-golden honey with a definite flavor and comes from the same plant responsible for many peoples' hay fever at the end of the summer. Goldenrod is an extremely prolific bloomer and an invaluable source of pollen and nectar for honey bees.

Heather honey (*Calluna vulgaris*) is produced a lot on the British Isles. It is a dark honey with a rich, complex, and persistent flavor and aroma.

Lavender honey (*Lavandula augustifolia*) is produced in southern France more than anywhere else in the world. It is a nearly white honey, with an intense but delicate lavender taste and a fruity aroma.

Milkweed honey (*Asclepias syriaca*) is produced in Michigan, where bees collect the herbal weed's very pale nectar. The honey is nearly white, with a slightly tangy flavor.

Mustard honey (*Sinapis alba*), also abundant in Europe, where acres and acres of yellow mustard bloom, is a creamy, ivory-colored honey. It is aromatic and persistent in flavor, and not overly sweet.

Rosemary honey (*Rosmarinus officinalis*) is made in southern Italy and other Mediterranean regions. It is very pale, nearly white in color, and has a delicate floral taste with a hint of bitter almond.

Sage honey (*Salvia*) is produced in California, where black button, white, and purple sage is abundant. It is very pale in color, with a fine, delicate flavor that is highly prized.

Thyme honey (*Thymus vulgaris*) is produced by bees anywhere that thyme grows wild and unimpeded, including Greece, Sicily, parts of Spain and France, and parts of the United States, to name a few. It is a light amber honey with a slightly spicy or minty flavor, considered by some to be the queen of all honeys.

Willow herb honey (*Epilobium augustifolium*), produced from willow herb, also called fireweed, grows in places where woods have been burnt down, particularly in the great northwest of the United States. Fireweed produces lovely pink blossoms all summer long. The honey is light amber with a slight floral taste.

Tannin in the plant's flower nectar is what gives dark honeys their color and stronger flavor.

Monofloral herbal honeys should be extracted and bottled by the beekeeper without the use of heat. Heating honey diminishes its natural flavor, natural volatile herbal oils, mineral content, and antibacterial qualities.

Keep growing herbs of all kinds, including dandelions in your lawn, and do not ever use pesticides or other chemical products on them! Honey bees, so essential to our human life, will repay you many times over with their delicious honeys.

Full Sun Spotlight

☙ by Elizabeth Barrette ❧

Many popular herbs come from sunny regions, such as the Mediterranean, which makes them ideal for gardens that get a great deal of direct sunlight. Native wildflowers that are common in desert or prairie habitats can be mixed in with your sun-loving herbs. It's better to grow plants that will be happy in the space you have rather than try to coddle delicate annuals that require extra water and supplemental shade.

Gardening Tricks

A sunny garden lets you take full advantage of the sun's power. When you establish your garden, think about your site and its characteristics. Its features, and your choice of plants, will determine what plants will thrive there. Sunny environments pose challenges, though.

Challenges of a Sunny Garden

Sunlight is a basic requirement for growing plants. However, too much of a good thing can make some plants struggle to survive. Gardens that get a lot of sunlight may suffer from problems due to their open location, such as:

Drought

Plants that grow in deserts, scrublands, savannas, and dry prairies are vulnerable to water loss. They must be able to store water, reach distant water, or resist water loss from evaporation.

Erosion

Plants that grow in desert and alpine habitats, open fields, and exposed slopes are especially vulnerable to erosion. Low-growing plants and those with tough fibrous root systems anchor the soil to prevent erosion.

Wind

Wind tears away soil and blossoms; it breaks branches and otherwise damages plants. Wind-resistant plants have narrow leaves and flexible branches. Many have creeping or mat forms that stay low to the ground.

Exposure

Sunny sites have little or no cover from trees, bushes, walls, or other barriers to block contaminants like salt or traffic exhaust. Plants should be tolerant to local impurities, perhaps with tough leaves and bark, or rigorous biochemistry.

Heat

Plants that grow in direct sun must be heat-tolerant. These plants may be tough and wiry, or fleshy and succulent. They often have silvery, hairy, or waxy leaves to resist the sun's fierce rays.

Designing Garden Spaces

Design covers all the underlying features of the garden that create its shape and character. Orientation is the relationship of the garden to other features, such as the sun. If you live where sunlight is rare or shallow, orient your garden to the sun. In the Northern Hemisphere, this means a south-facing, flat or sloped area. If your sunny days are frequent and the sun is strong, you might choose an eastern- or western-orientation to soften the rays.

Hardscaping, which is landscaping with rock, wood, and so forth, includes all the things you build, such as raised beds or pathways. A sunny alpine garden might benefit from terraces to slow erosion, while a desert garden could use pale stone paths to reflect heat. Decorations illustrate a garden's theme. Celebrate the sun's power with a sundial, a golden gazing ball, sun faces on a wall, statues of solar deities, or similar imagery.

Water-retention features are important because of evaporation. Sunny gardens tend to dry out faster than shady gardens. Compensate by adding water-retention features. Dig a hole to bury a log or other organic matter. Dig small, shallow trenches called swales that catch water as it flows down a slope. Swales also help slow soil erosion. Plants situated near buried organic matter or swales benefit from a much higher "effective rainfall," because they can tap into water trapped in these areas. If you want to plant herbs with higher water needs than your area rainfall provides, this is the place to put them.

Wind barriers reduce the force of air movement through your garden. In a small space, you could choose a slatted or latticed fence to slow the wind. Now, you have a place to plant some vines, too! A larger garden might have room for a windbreak made of bushes or even trees. Think of the beautiful twisted shapes of hardy plants in windswept deserts or mountainsides. As they break up the wind, your bushes or trees can turn into "wind sculptures" themselves.

New plants need some protection from the elements until they become established. Plan to provide supplemental water to perennials for the first growing season, bushes for two, and trees for three. They may also benefit from temporary shade, either a solid sheet blocking just the midday sun, or a partial filter affecting more hours. A little extra water or shade can also save a plant that starts to wilt.

For best results, layer the plants in your garden. This lets your sun-loving herbs get plenty of light so they don't accidentally shade each other, but it also lets you tuck a few plants underneath that have a lower tolerance of heat, salt, wind, or other stress factors. Dense, layered plantings work more like natural ecosystems, making them easier to maintain and more attractive to wildlife.

Herbs for Sunny Places

Most herbs require full sun six or more hours every day. Some do well in as little as three hours of sunlight. However, not all herb plants can tolerate the hot, dry conditions of full exposure to the sun. Your best bet, of course, is to shop for plants native to your area. Many wildflowers are also herbs, and also check for herbs that originated in desert, scrub, or prairie habitats. Resources on xericulture (landscaping for hot dry areas) or permaculture (landscaping that mimics natural ecosystems) may help you design a terrific sunny herb garden. All of the plants listed below thrive on abundant direct sunlight; related tolerances are also listed. If you want to find more, seek plants with the following traits that suit them for life under the sun:

- Narrow leaves or needles
- Woolly, hairy, or prickly leaves
- Thick, succulent leaves or stems
- Waxy coating on leaves or stems
- Resinous or oily leaves, stems, or bark
- Silvery, grayish, or bluish foliage
- Long taproot for reaching deep water
- Wide, dense, shallow root system for gathering water over great range
- Huge globular root, or root nodules, for storing water and nutrients

Aloe

Aloe (*Aloe spp.*) has dozens of species that offer different shapes and colors. The medicinal herb aloe vera is a well-known treatment for sunburn and other minor burns, but give the plant extra water if you harvest its gel. Aloe tolerates drought, extreme heat, high salt, sandy soil, and wind.

Artemesia

Artemisia (*Artemisia spp.*) has silvery or grayish leaves that come in various shapes. Mugwort is thought to have magical qualities, to enhance dreams and psychic abilities, while wormwood deters pests. Artemisia tolerates drought and wind. Silver mound and big sagebrush also tolerate extreme heat.

Bay Laurel

Bay laurel (*Laurus nobilis*) is a handsome tree with dark glossy green leaves that can be dried for flavoring soups or other recipes. Bay laurel was thought to have magical uses related to success and creativity. Excellent small tree helps create a layered garden. It tolerates drought and heat.

Bayberry

Bayberry (*Myrica cerifera*) has aromatic leaves and berries that provide scent for candles or other crafts. Berries attract wildlife. The root bark has medicinal qualities for skin conditions. Bayberry makes an excellent hedge, and it tolerates drought, poor soil (sand or clay), salt, and wind.

Beebalm

Beebalm (*Monarda didyma* or *M. fistulosa*) has dark-green leaves and scarlet, purple, or pink flowers that insects and hummingbirds love. Edible and medicinal, this plant is especially favored for making tea. It tolerates mild drought, heat, and wind.

Bougainvillea

Bougainvillea (*Bougainvillea spp.*) is a vigorous vine that bears inconspicuous flowers surrounded by leaf bracts in shades of scarlet, orange, yellow, purple, or pink. It makes a vivid display against a wall or fence; thorny varieties also discourage unwanted traffic. It tolerates heat, drought, pollution, and salt.

Cedar

Cedar (*Thuja occidentalis* or *T. plicata*) is sacred in some traditions. Cedar is used in aromatherapy, and its wood and oil discourage pests. Different varieties make good specimen trees or evergreen hedges. It tolerates drought, heat, poor soil, and wind. Eastern red cedar is salt-tolerant.

Chives

Chives (*Allium schoenoprasum*) has tubular leaves that grow in clumps. It produces pink or purple pom-pom flowers. Both leaves and flowers are edible and have a mild onion flavor. The scent discourages pests; the plant tolerates mild drought conditions and poor soil.

Epazote

Epazote (*Chenopodium ambrosioides*) is a large bushy herb with jagged leaves; it produces many yellow flowers. Cooked with beans, a small amount of epazote discourages flatulence. Burned on a fire, it repels insects. It is tolerant of heat and poor soil.

Ephedra

Ephedra (*Ephedra sinica*) has leaves that reduce to tiny scales, which make this herb look like a big bundle of twigs. Its medicinal uses include allergy control and appetite reduction. It grows well in desert or mountainous habitats and is tolerant of drought, extreme heat, sandy, or gravelly soil.

Fig

Fig (*Ficus carica*) has both wild fig and domestic varieties. Wild fig trees are quite tall, while domestic varieties are usually small trees or shrubs. Brown turkey, conadria, and black mission produce excellent fruit that is attractive to humans and wildlife. The fruit is highly nutritious and a gentle laxative. Fig trees tolerate drought, heat, poorly drained or infertile soil, and sandy or rocky soil.

Garlic

Garlic (*Allium sativum*) produces thick, fleshy bulbs underground, and the more sun a garlic plant receives the bigger bulbs it will produce! Delicious used in cooking, garlic also boosts immunity, kills microbes, and discourages pests in the garden and elsewhere. It tolerates drought and moderate heat.

Germander

Germander (*Teucrium chamaedrys* or *T. fruiticans*) is good for hedges and its flowers attract bees. Wall germander makes a low hedge, ideal for knotwork herb gardens. Bush germander forms large rounded mounds. It is used to treat skin conditions, colds, and fevers. It tolerates drought, heat, and poor or stony soil.

Honeysuckle

Honeysuckle (*Lonicera spp.*) is available in bush form, which makes a terrific hedge, and in vine forms that are ideal for fences or trellises. Its intensely sweet flowers attract insects, and its berries appeal to birds. It tolerates drought and heat. Cape honeysuckle is also salt-tolerant.

Horehound

Horehound (*Marrubium vulgare*) has beautiful crinkled leaves that are protected by a wooly covering. Horehound is made into delicious candy that soothes sore throat or cough; it also is used to make cough syrup and tea. The plant tolerates drought, poor sandy soil, and a wide pH range.

Hyssop

Hyssop (*Hyssopus officinalis*) has fragrant leaves and flowers that attract bees and butterflies. Hyssop tea treats cold and flu and soothes the stomach. It tolerates drought and poor soil.

Juniper

Juniper (*Juniperus spp.*) is an evergreen bush or tree that produces scaled or spiky leaves. Both a male and female plant are needed if the dark berries are to be produced. The berries have a delicious resinous flavor that is useful for dark meats, pickling brine, gin, and other liquors. Juniper tolerates alpine conditions, drought, heat, and wind to control erosion. Bar Harbor juniper also tolerates salt.

Lavender

Lavender (*Lavandula angustifolia* or *L. officinalis*) produces purple flowers on gray-green stems, which make this plant both fragrant and beautiful. Use it in crafts or body care products. It tolerates drought, heat, poor soil, and wind. The compact forms tolerate moderate alpine conditions.

Mullein

Mullein (*Verbascum thapsus*) has soft green leaves and spikes of yellow flowers. It makes a good plant dye and has medicinal qualities. It tolerates drought, heat, and poor soil (chalk, gravel, and sand).

Oak

Oak (*Quercus spp.*) has bark that is used for tanning and dyeing. The acorns are edible, and it tolerates drought well. Holm, live oak, red or white oak, and willow oak are salt-tolerant. Holm oak tolerates pollution and wind. Live oak and scrub oak control erosion.

Olive

Olive (*Olea europaea*) is a small tree with leathery green leaves; it bears edible fruit and is an excellent source for oil. Olive was sacred in Greco-Roman and other traditions. It tolerates mild drought, heat, and moderate salt.

Passionflower

Passionflower (*Passiflora incarnata*) is a woody vine that produces spectacular purple or pink flowers and edible fruit. Its medicinal uses include treatments for anxiety and insomnia. It tolerates drought, heat, and sandy or gravelly soil.

Pine

Pine (*Pinus spp.*) is an evergreen tree or bush that grows in variety of shapes and is adapted to various conditions. The penetrating scent makes pine useful for some respiratory complaints. It tolerates alpine conditions, drought, and wind. Japanese black pine is salt-tolerant. Choose Coulter, Jeffrey, or Ponderosa pine for erosion control.

Poppy

Poppy (*Papaver spp.*) has fuzzy, jagged, gray-green leaves and brilliant red, orange, or yellow flowers. It is drought-tolerant. Iceland poppy also tolerates chilly alpine conditions and wind.

Purple Coneflower

Purple coneflower (*Echinacea purpurea*) is a bushy prairie plant that has narrow pointed leaves and pink or pale purple flowers. The flowers attract butterflies and its seeds attract birds. It tolerates drought, heat, and wind.

Rose

Rose (*Rosa spp.*, especially *rugosa*) has dark green leaves, thorny stems, and red, pink, yellow, or white flowers. Rosehips make excellent jelly high in vitamin C. Roses tolerate drought, heat, pollution, salt, sandy soil, and wind.

Rosemary

Rosemary (*Rosmarinus officinalis*) has needle-like leaves that have a strong resinous flavor when dried, which makes them useful in cooking. The plant tolerates heat and salt. Prostrate rosemary controls erosion and tolerates slopes.

Rue

(*Ruta graveolens*) has a delicate appearance due to its rounded bluish leaflets. Rue repels pests. It tolerates moderate drought, heat, slopes, salt, and sandy or clay soils.

Sage

Sage (*Salvia officinalis*) bears leathery gray-green leaves and blue or purple flowers on woody stems. Leaves are used in cooking and aid digestion. Sage tolerates drought, heat, and slopes. Groundcover salvias, such as 'Gracias' or 'Bees Bliss,' are especially good for erosion control.

Santolina

Santolina (*Santolina chamaecyparissus*) has nubbly silver-gray foliage that produces tiny yellow flowers. When dried, it appears in everlasting bouquets and fragrant sachets. It tolerates drought and extreme heat.

Thyme

Thyme (*Thymus spp.*) has tiny leaves that form mats or miniature bushes with white or pink flowers. The fresh or dried leaves are used in cooking. It tolerates drought, foot traffic, heat, and wind. Creeping or mat forms control erosion and tolerate chilly alpine conditions.

Witch Hazel

Witch hazel (*Hamamelis virginiana*) produces yellow flowers on bushes in earliest spring. An astringent herb, it is used for skin conditions. It tolerates drought and salt.

Yarrow

Yarrow (*Achillea millefolium*) produces fragrant, ferny leaves that bear panicles of white or yellow flowers. Yarrow tea is used for female complaints. It tolerates chilly alpine conditions, drought, mild salt, and wind. Controls erosion.

Fertilizers for Free

≫ by Janice Sharkey ≪

I t's easy to spend money on tempting ornaments, plants, and tools for the garden. I'm always looking for ways to economize, so my ears pricked up when I heard about composting—making fertilizers for free. The idea appealed to me because making compost could save me money. The idea of composting also satisfied my urge to recycle and reduce my carbon footprint. I could produce fertile soil and at the same time reap the rewards of greater yields. But, surely, having free fertilizer could not be that simple I thought; and at first, it was not. Like any good detective, I had to ask some basic questions about why, what, where, and most importantly, how to compost.

Composting

Why not let nature do its job and leave it well alone? One reason to increase fertility is to maximize gardens for both crops and abundant flowering. Compost heaps are not the most attractive objects in the garden, but what they contain is very beneficial to the soil and wildlife. Homemade compost is great for improving bad soil. Whether the soil is compacted or poor in nutrients, compost will almost certainly help to improve it. It also encourages strong, healthy growth in plants. Not only does it feed plants immediately, it liberates more fertility from the soil, and it carries an incredible range of micro-organisms that protect plants from all those nasty pests and diseases.

Where Are the Free Fertilizers?

A steady supply of free soil can be produced just from composting kitchen and garden waste (things that came from the soil). Using the homemade, brown, crumbly matter on beds and border is a must. It will develop a community of "mini beasts" to help in the waste-decaying process. Bigger beasts—mice, hedgehogs, and slow worms—might make their home in compost heaps, too. A compost heap is warm and holds some favorite goods, such as big juicy worms, slugs, and spiders that are appetizing to some other animals.

Where to Locate a Compost Heap

You need to place your compost bin or heap directly onto the soil to allow worms to get in. Most soil also holds microbes that can be found in massive numbers in your compost heap. Some microbes will attack the humus when added to garden soil and combine these raw materials with water and nitrogen from the air to increase fertility.

All that natural decomposed goodness will heat up the soil-rich microbes and release benefits to plants.

What to Put in Compost

A balanced mix of ingredients needs to go into a compost heap to ensure usable compost from green waste. Things that are good to add include: teabags, kitchen waste, old plant foliage (minus the seed heads of weeds), and brown waste (shredded, woody prunings; leaves, cardboard, or straw).

How to Start Compost

When you begin to compost waste, you need to make sure that you build it up properly; otherwise, you could hit on a couple of problems. You can add as much green waste as you want, as long as it is a good mixture of everything. Brown waste should be added in thin layers. (A thick layer may not rot down very quickly.) I sieve my compost before using it to make it uniform. Then, I use it as a mulch or top dressing, but not where seedling weeds could be a problem. I could steam kill the weed seeds within, but I find this too costly a job in time and electricity. So rather than make more work for myself, I brew compost tea, which eliminates weed seeds because the tea is too rich for them.

Compost Tea

By placing a small bag of compost muck into, say, a pair of old tights and placing in a bucket of rainwater it will make stewed compost but kill off the weed seed. Compost does not just feed the soil; it fires it up with all sorts of microbes. Extracts of compost show real benefits to almost every plant and especially by using liquid extracts that can even be sprayed onto plants to reduce pest and diseases.

Compost tea, an extract of living entities, consists of all sorts of fungi, bacteria and other microscopic creatures. When this soup is added to potting compost or soil, the plants become much healthier and more able to resist pests and diseases. A bag of mulch can remain effective for weeks as it leaches out soluble fertility. But within a few days or so, many living organisms in compost will have been drowned. It is better to make smaller "tea bags" and change them at least once a week. Of course, used bags can be emptied and the washed compost can still be used. It still retains a lot of value despite leaching its nutrients into the water. And better still, most of the weed seeds in it will have drowned. You could go one step further and give your garden a well-earned "tea break." Liquid extracts from good compost can act as a spray on fertilizer.

Special Brews

In olden days, many gardeners made and used simple plant teas served for vegetables and those few plants kept in pots. But not all plants need the same nutrients and when more people started to grow tomatoes, they discovered these crops needed a feed richer in potassium (potash), especially when grown in pots. So the hunt was on for a plant rich in potash. It was Lawrence Hills who promoted the benefits of comfrey (*Symphytum officinale*). Some call it a weed, as it grows widely in damp places. Hills suggested steeping the leaves and stems in water. The results are similar to commercial tomato feeds.

Comfrey Is Terrific Fertilizer

Once comfrey plants are established in your garden, the leaves can be cut three or four times yearly and used in a variety of ways. You could add to the compost heap to speed up decomposition, or use as a mulch to feed tomatoes, runner beans, squashes, cucumbers, peppers and soft fruits. They are great around blackcurrant bushes and can boost your strawberry harvest with a comfrey-mulch. Comfrey also deters slugs. Comfrey leaves release their nutrients quickly when placed directly on the soil, and comfrey mulch can be used in potato trenches, tomato planting holes, and for some legumes. Try adding chopped comfrey leaves to leaf mold, which helps it to rot down to the same black liquid that is produced when making a liquid feed. The leaf mold absorbs this nutrient-rich liquid, and can be used in potting composts or as mulch.

Comfrey Is Good, Borage Might Be Better

Not all plants want such high levels of potash, and some may suffer if you stick only to comfrey as a liquid fertilizer. Scorching, yellowing, and worse can be a result of magnesium shortage induced by excessive potassium. Adding urine (which acts as another free fertilizer) is not a cure as it is also rich in potash. Instead, add lots of borage leaves—an annual that is easy to grow and which bees really love. Make liquid feed entirely from the leaves to solve this problem. Borage leaves and stems rot down to make a feed with similar nutrients to comfrey but with more magnesium. As borage can be grown as a temporary crop anywhere and even over-wintered for an earlier harvest, it is even more convenient than the perennial comfrey—and slightly less revolting. But best of all, borage makes a better balanced liquid feed for a greater variety of plants.

Leaf Mold

Leaf mold is free for the taking every fall. The leaves decay on the ground to form a rich, dark material that is excellent as a soil improver. It is used as a low-fertility soil conditioner and as a mulch to retain moisture, usually leaving leaves to decompose for a year. If you want to add the leaf mold to seed and potting mixes, it has to become a more crumbly, darker consistency, which takes about two years to decompose. Leaf mold has many uses, such as acting as a mulch blanket to protect the crowns of tender plants like penstemons. It will do two things: keep off frost in the winter and retain moisture in the summer. To make a more nutrient-rich material for use in a potting mix, add comfrey leaves to one-year-old leaf mold and allow them to decay together for a few months. It can also be used as a top dressing for grass by mixing leaf mold with loam and sand and sprinkling over the top of a lawn.

Grow Green Manure

These are plants grown to improve the soil by creating a blanket that can not only suppress weeds but also release nutrients into the soil, which are excellent for opening up heavy earth and improving light soils. You can either dig in the crop, usually in early spring, or go for the no-dig technique. This means simply cutting plants down and leaving the foliage on the surface to decompose. You can plant through this layer, treating it exactly as mulch, or move it to one side before sowing seeds. Alternatively, cut, remove, and compost. There is a range of green manures, including alfalfa, fenugreek, lupine, and mustard seed. Some you sow in spring, others in late summer or early fall for over-wintering. Some green manures, such as lupines, fix nitrogen, while others, like rye, do not.

Garden Compost Is Free

While "there's no free lunch," you could grow yours if you use free fertilizers and seeds collected in last year's harvest. Then, let Mother Nature do the rest. What's more, compost adds to the earth. I can never get enough new compost in my garden!

Herb Q and A

by JD Hortwort

Herbs are among the easiest plants to grow given the right location, soil, and sunlight. But they can still present problems, as these questions from gardeners reveal.

Q: The oregano I planted three years ago is growing well, but its flavor seems less intense. What might have caused it to lose its potency?

A: Herbs, especially culinary herbs like oregano, are valued for the intense flavors or aromas they impart to foods. Without sufficient quantities of the essential oils herbs are known for, they are just ornamentals. When an herb loses strength, one of several things may be going on.

First, check to see that your herbs are getting at least eight hours of quality sunlight each day. Dappled sunlight won't do. Herbs create their essential oils in what most flowering annuals would consider harsh conditions like glaring, all-day sun. If your herb patch is getting less sunlight than necessary, consider moving the plants to a better location.

Next, take a look at the soil the herb is planted in. Herbs like what gardeners call "lean" soil. Too much organic material can make most herbs weak, in structure and in flavor.

Finally (and this is in the same vein), ask yourself if you are over-fertilizing. Annual flowers and most garden vegetables like regular feedings with a balanced fertilizer at least once a month. Herbs prefer less fertilizer, whether you are using organic or man-made products. Treat them like perennials. Feed then with a general-purpose fertilizer on installation and once mid-season. If you have established plants, feed them early in the season, when they break dormancy, and again at mid-season. That will be plenty.

Q: Are there any herbs that I can grow in the shade?

A: Sadly, most of the culinary herbs we use—basil, thyme, sage, marjoram, cilantro, garlic, etc.—need at least six to eight hours of sunlight daily to do well. An exception is parsley, which seems to grow well in dappled sunlight, such as found under a tall tree, or in 4 to 6 hours of direct sunlight.

A safe way to grow mint is in the shade. I use the word "safe," because mint grown in full sun can quickly overrun a plant bed. Mint includes peppermint and spearmint, as well as other plants in the mint family, like lemon balm and bee balm. Sweet woodruff, a vanilla-scented herb used to flavor wine, is another herb that prefers shade. A relatively new herb being grown in the United States is culantro (*Eryngium foe-tidum*). Although it is not related to cilantro, culantro smells and tastes just like cilantro. The difference is that culantro prefers moist shade.

Q: What's the difference between annual and perennial herbs?

A: Annuals of any sort complete their growing cycle in one season. At some point in that season, the plant will begin to flower, make seeds, and then die. You can prolong the life of an annual herb by keeping the flowers pinched off. Perennial herbs may die to the ground in the winter, but they come back for at least three years. They may flower, but flowering doesn't mark the end of their growth cycle. In fact, some perennial herbs, such as rosemary, can live for decades. Perennial herbs and some annuals can be grown indoors for the winter. However, like their annual cousins, they need plenty of bright light and steady temperatures to keep them producing until they can be set outside again next season.

Q: Which is better for my herbs, organic or inorganic fertilizers?

A: This is a debate that can really kick up a fuss. Some gardeners have no preference. Others passionately argue against the use of man-made fertilizer. It should be established at the onset that herbs don't like a lot of fertilizer—regardless of the kind. Too much may cause abundant growth, but that growth will be weak and cause the plant to be more susceptible to disease and insects. The amount of essential oils will be reduced as well, so your herbs will not be as aromatic or as flavorful as you would like.

As to which is better, each type of fertilizer has its pluses and minuses. Fertilizers are meant to add nutrients to the soil that are needed by plants to grow. The nutrients in organic fertilizers come from some living source. They can be animal manure, fish meal, blood or bone meal, or seaweed extract. Some gardeners consider ordinary compost to be sufficient fertilizer. The point is, organic fertilizers are natural by-products that will tend to be more easily incorporated into the soil. Organic fertilizers usually will not cause damage to native earthworms and other critters that work to break down your soil. This is important because those critters are necessary to break down organic fertilizers to make the nutrients within available to plants. On the other hand, they can be messy if you are trying to gather your own from the barnyard. Gathering manure while it is still "green" is not only messy, you can burn the plants you apply it around. If you are purchasing processed organic fertilizers, you have to be careful that your fertilizer has any nutritional value at all. Sometimes, processing takes all of the benefit out of the fertilizer.

Commercial (man-made) fertilizers are easily available and come in multiple formulas, allowing you to customize your application specifically to the plant you are feeding. Because they are mass produced, they tend to be less expensive. Some commercial fertilizers are formulated to be released over time, making it unnecessary to schedule a repeat feeding. On the other hand, it's easier to make a mistake and over-apply commercial fertilizers. Man-made fertilizers are actually salts. Once they mix with water, the nutrients are instantly available, which increases the risk of burning the plants you want to feed. A less dire consequence is rapid growth, followed by a lull—not unlike getting a sugar rush that is followed by a sugar crash. Commercial fertilizers can build up in the soil and create a toxic condition. Organic fertilizers are unlikely to cause this problem.

Finally, man-made fertilizers come from primarily from petroleum. There is hardly a more sensitive topic around than the consequences of humankind's dependence on petroleum. For this reason alone, many gardeners prefer not to use commercial fertilizers.

As you weigh the options of organic versus inorganic, keep in mind that both types of fertilizer, when properly used, provide the same nutrients to the plant. Whichever you choose to use, be responsible in the application.

Q: My rosemary topiary has mildew on it. What should I spray it with?

A: Let's get to the root of the problem on your rosemary. It's not mildew. It's spider mites. Spider mites chew on the rosemary and excrete honeydew. This, in turn, is a growing medium for the mildew. Get rid of the insect and you get rid of the mildew.

Q: I didn't think insects would bother herbs. What can I spray on my herbs to get rid of the bugs that won't keep me from eating my plants?

A: I'm not sure there is such a thing as a plant that a bug won't eat. Practically every plant has some sort of insect that likes to munch on it. The best "insecticide" available is a properly grown, healthy plant. A number of studies have been done that indicate plants that are set in the right soil, in the right location and provided with the right nutrients (either naturally in the soil or supplemented with fertilizer), will not be attractive to bugs. If a few bugs do take a nibble, the plant is strong enough to survive without intervention.

Alas, life isn't perfect—even in the garden. Sometimes, we have to intervene or risk losing our investment. Early intervention is the key. Treat when you first see signs of damage. Surprisingly, a strong spray of water will work to eliminate minor bug populations. Repeat as necessary. Of course, you better have your herbs planted in well-drained soil or root rot might be the next problem you incur.

The next weapon in your arsenal is insecticidal soap. Insecticidal soaps are made of fatty acids, something bugs hate. You can buy insecticidal soaps, or make your own. The Internet has hundreds of recipes and most rely on the use of non-detergent bar soap made without dyes or perfumes. Dissolve a five-ounce bar of soap in two quarts of water. You can grate the soap and dissolve it in boiling water, or you can just let the bar naturally dissolve in a jar of warm water over several days. Use 2 tablespoons of the solution to one quart of water and spray as needed.

Q: Can I eat the wild herbs that come up in my lawn and around my property?

A: Maybe. Do you know for a fact that no chemicals have been used to treat the plants? Has something been sprayed on those plants or around them? If there is any doubt about what has been put out around the plants, then no— you should not eat them. The other qualifier is, are you sure you know what you might be eating? People use angelica (*Angelica archangelica*) stems for candying. But angelica looks a lot like wild hemlock (*Conium maculatum*), which can be deadly. Your best bet is to find someone who can teach you what is and is not safe to consume in the wild. Or just grow its cultivated cousin.

Plants Need Friends, Too

by Misty Kuceris

Nature is wonderful, and its diversity is marvelous. As we learn to understand what we see, we can begin to realize how the balance that is created keeps the world alive and vibrant. The shallow-rooted maple trees bring up moisture so that other plants can absorb this water. The fragrant flowers attract bees, which provide growth to other plants through the process of pollination. Small, cluster flowers attract beneficial insects to the garden that will attack the crop-destroying pests. Even frogs and other invertebrates that find nourishment in shallow pools of water help nature to maintain its diversity and balance.

Our homes can be beautiful sanctuaries away from the tensions of the world, and beautiful landscapes and gardens can enhance our sanctuaries. All too often, however, landscapers and gardeners forget about the importance of diversity in yards. Too many plantings from the same plant families create monocultures. Without diversity, the potential beauty of thriving, living environments can, instead, become sterile canvases.

Worse, the belief in using pesticides when plants are stressed, diseased, or injured is strong. While using pesticides may take care of the immediate problem, it does little to correct the situation. In fact, the overuse of any chemical can create a chain reaction of new problems: Beneficial insects are lost; run-off pollutes watersheds and other land; and potential danger for living creatures, including humans, increases.

In reality, the world—the entire universe—is a living, breathing organism that strives to work together in an organic way that creates balance in life. Everything has a purpose, and nature is the best example of that purpose. For you, the gardener, the best way to maintain this diversity and be a part of this living organism is to learn about companion planting and the incredible contribution made by herbs.

The Iroquois and other Native Americans recognized the world as a living organism. One of the most famous stories of companion planting is found in the Iroquois creation story: "The Three Sisters." In this story, Sky Woman looked through a hole in the sky and fell through. She would have landed in the sea. However, animals took the soil from the bottom of the sea and placed it on the back of a large turtle. She was able to land on a safe place, Turtle Island, which is now called North America.

Sky Woman was pregnant when she fell and gave birth to a daughter. When the daughter was a young woman, she became pregnant by the West Wind. Unfortunately, the daughter died while giving birth to twin boys and was buried by Sky Woman in the soil. Three sacred plants grew from her grave: corn, beans, and squash—"the three sisters." The sons and all of humanity were provided with food, which kept them alive.

Corn is still considered one of the most important crops in North America. The combination of corn, beans, and squash is packed with vitamins and minerals that provide a near-to-perfect meal. In addition to its nutrients, this combination has value in other ways. Less land is used for planting, because beans can climb up the corn for support. It has a symbiotic relationship with rhizobium bacteria (bacteria that fixes nitrogen in the soil). This means that the beans can actually use the nitrogen in the air and replenish the soil. The squash leaves cover the earth and become a living mulch. They provide weed control in two ways: by blocking sunlight from the ground and through chemical secretions (allelopathy) from the plant that have an adverse affect on weeds. Finally, squash, because it provides protection from the sun, conserves water.

Austrian philosopher Rudolf Steiner understood that the world is a living organism and a small part of the greater cosmos. A group of farmers approached Steiner in the early 1920s because they were concerned about the health of their livestock as well as the decline of their crops. In 1924, Steiner held a series of lectures at Koberwitz, Germany, which would became the fundamental principles of biodynamic farming. In biodynamic farming, the soil and the farm are living organisms. Farms need to be self-contained and soil needs to be continually improved. Cover crops, green manure, and crop diversification are part of the process. Companion planting is important so that plants can support each other. From Steiner's work, Demeter International was formed in 1928 to create the Demeter Biodynamic® Farm Standard.

When Ehrenfried Pfeiffer was nineteen years old, he met Steiner and began a long association with him. In the 1930s, Pfeiffer lectured in the United States. It was when he worked at Philadelphia's Hahnemann Medical College that he experimented with using crystallization patterns of blood for the diagnosis of cancer. Eventually, he used crystallization testing to determine which plants would interact well with each other. From this testing, he developed chromatograms of various plants, both individually and in combination. His conclusions: Clear and bright chromatograms formed from mixtures of plants meant that the plants made good companion plants. Cloudy or dull chromatograms indicated the plants were not compatible. He attempted to use science to determine which plants were best in companion planting.

Today, research into companion planting is being conducted by various colleges, universities, and government organizations. At the Agricultural Research Service (ARS), United States Department of Agriculture (USDA), you'll find that research focuses on the use of cover crops to increase nitrogen in the soil or crop output for biofuels, as well as research on the use of plants and herbs as pesticides.

One of the most interesting and recent research projects involves geraniums as a companion plant. On March 8, 2010, ARS, USDA released the findings of a study that showed geraniums can be valuable in controlling the Japanese beetle (*Popillia japonica*). This insect costs the ornamental plant industry in the United States over $450 million in damage each year. The Japanese beetle feeds on over 300 plant species, including ornamental plants, soybean, maize, fruits, and vegetables. When the Japanese beetle eats the petals of a geranium, it becomes paralyzed for several hours. This gives birds a chance to eat the beetle before it recovers.

As you can see, companion planting is more than an old-world concept. It is a system in which you study your environment and determine which plants work together to help each other. It's a system where you can intersperse vegetables with flowering plants and sprinkle an assortment of herbs throughout. The benefits to companion planting are enormous.

You increase the diversity of your garden and landscape, providing plants, trees, and shrubs a better opportunity to live out a healthy life. By providing them with a better life, you put more nutrients back into the soil, use fewer pesticides (if any at all), create a habitat for all living creatures, and create a healthier environment for you and your family.

You attract insects and other living creatures, which can aid plants in your yard. Some of these insects aid your yard by attracting pests and keeping them from attacking and destroying the plants. Other insects attack and kill the pests that can destroy your plants.

You can increase the nitrogen in your soil by planting certain crops, such as peas, beans, and clover, which have the ability to take nitrogen out of the air and put it into the soil. These plants are able to do this by interacting with the rhizobium bacteria.

You can suppress pests through chemical reactions with certain plants. The best known plant for this is the African marigold. This flowering plant releases thiopene, which is a nematode repellent. Nematodes in the soil can cause damage to plant roots. The most famous plant that exudes an allelochemical is the black walnut tree. Even the Romans knew that planting anything near a black walnut tree could be deadly. The tree releases juglone, a toxin, to surrounding plants. Yet, the planting of rye could be beneficial because its allelochemical prevents weed formation.

You can create more space in your garden and landscape while also protecting plants and decreasing the amount of water you use. This is done through planting short plants under taller plants, such as squash or pumpkin under corn, or planting oats with alfalfa.

The most frequent use of companion planting is found in vegetable gardens, but if you don't want to grow vegetables, you can still put in companion plants for your flowering garden. You can even put in companion plants for various trees and shrubs.

Soil is always the first place to start if you want a good garden. Add African marigolds (*Tagetes erecta*) and French marigolds to repel any soil nematodes. You can add other marigolds (*Calendula*) as well, because they repel insects. Caraway (*Carum carvi*) is a very important herb for any garden. With its long taproot, it loosens the soil for better drainage and pulls up nutrients from the subsoil. Lovage (*Levisticum officinale*) and marjoram (*Origanum majorana*) improve the health of most plants.

Pest insects are a problem for any garden. While they may not totally destroy your plants, they can poke holes or suck the chlorophyll out of the leaves and destroy the beauty of your garden. The most common pest is the aphid. However, there are other pests such as Japanese beetles, slugs, and snails. While ants may seem to be a common pest in gardens, ants usually appear when there are aphids. Aphids leave a sweet substance, called honeydew, which attracts the ants.

Nasturtiums (*Tropaeolum spp.*) deter aphids and are a wonderful addition to your salad. Any members of the Allium family (onions, garlic, and leeks) are good hosts for beneficial wasps. Coriander (*Coriandrum sativum*) also repels aphids. However, do not plant it near fennel (*Foeniculum vulgare, F. vulgare dulce*). By planting tansy (*Tanacetum vulgare*) and pennyroyal (*Mentha pulegium*) or (*Hedeoma pulegioides*), you'll deter the ants.

Slugs and snails are repelled by rosemary (*Rosmarinus officinalis*) when you spread the branches throughout the garden. They are also repelled by thyme (*Thymus vulgaris, T. serpyllum*) or lavender (*Lavandula spp.*) planted around the border of your garden.

Other herbs are good for the garden because they repel a number of pests. These herbs include tarragon (*Artemisia dracunculus*), lavender (*Lavandula spp.*), oregano (*Origanum spp.*), and Catnip (*Nepeta cataria*). You can spread the branches of catnip throughout the garden to repel aphids, flea beetles, spittlebugs, ants, Japanese beetles, the Colorado potato beetle, and weevils. However, because catnip is so effective, it could also repel some of the beneficial insects that you want in your garden. Of course, catnip will also attract cats, which might help prevent some pests—moles and voles, for example. If you want to plant catnip in your garden, be very careful. It is highly invasive and can overtake other plants. Simply put it in a pot and plant the pot in your garden. This will keep the roots in check.

Attracting beneficial insects, such as praying mantis and lady beetles, can help prevent problems with other insects. Dill (*Anethum graveolens*), parsley (*Petroselinum crispum; P. hortense; P. sativum*), coriander (*Coriandrum sativum*), and angelica (*Angelica archangelica, A. atropurpurea, A. sinensis*) all have small flowers that attract these insects to your garden.

The best way to use these herbs is to intersperse them throughout your various flowering plants. Be very careful with angelica, however, as the fresh roots are poisonous. Also, it's easy to confuse angelica with water hemlock (*Cicuta maculate*), which is an extremely poisonous plant. One thing to remember about coriander, also known as cilantro, is that it bolts and flowers very quickly when the weather gets hot and humid.

When you decide that you want to plant vegetables, think of diversity again. Using herbs as companion plants benefit the vegetable garden in many of the same ways that they benefit your flowering garden. One advantage to companion planting is that some of the herbs will actually improve the taste of certain vegetables.

A favorite among gardeners is the tomato plant. When you plant bee balm (*Monarda didyma*) or sweet basil (*Ocimum basilicum*) with tomato plants, you improve the taste of tomatoes. And planting basil with tomatoes will repel mosquitoes and flies, as well as the tomato hornworm. Planting borage (*Borago Officinalis*) near tomatoes will also deter the tomato hornworm. Nasturtiums (*Tropaeolum spp.*) are good because they deter aphids. Chives (*Allium schoenoprasum*) is a good companion plant for tomatoes, as is sage (*Salvia officinalis*).

Dill (*Anethum graveolens*) is actually a trap plant for the tomato hornworm, but be careful with dill and do not plant it too close to tomatoes, as it could reduce their growth. Do not plant tansy (*Tanacetum vulgare*) near tomatoes.

There are many companion plants that improve the health and taste of plants in the cabbage family (broccoli, brussels sprouts, cabbage, cauliflower, Chinese cabbage, kale, and kohlrabi). Chamomile (*Charmaemelum nobile*) and garlic (*Allium sativum*) improve the growth and taste of cabbage. Dill (*Anethum graveolens*) also improves its growth and vitality. However, do not plant chamomile near carrots. Hyssop (*Hyssopus officinalis*), sage (*Salvia officinalis*), and rosemary (*Rosmarinus officinalis*) deter cabbage moths. Catnip (*Nepeta cataria*) and mint (*Mentha spp.*) also deter the white cabbage moth, but be very careful when planting either of these. They are extremely invasive. You might want to plant them in a container and place the entire container in the ground to prevent the roots from spreading. Nasturtium (*Tropaeolum spp.*) helps with the health of cabbages. It also deters beetles, aphids, whiteflies, and other cabbage pests. Members of the Allium family (onions, garlic, and leeks) deter aphids. While tansy (*Tanacetum vulgare*) deters cabbage worms and cutworms and is a good companion plant to most members of the cabbage family, it is not a good companion plant for kohlrabi.

Chives (*Allium cerefolium*) and flax improve the growth and flavor of carrots. Rosemary (*Rosmarinus officinalis*) and sage (*Salvia officinalis*) are good companion plants for carrots because they deter the carrot fly. However, never plant dill (*Anethum graveolens*) around carrots, because dill retards the growth of carrots.

Nasturtiums (*Tropaeolum spp.*) deter beetles, aphids, whiteflies, striped cucumber beetles, and other pests of the cucurbit family, making it a wonderful companion plant for cucumbers. However, do not plant aromatic herbs, such as sage (*Salvia officinalis*), near cucumbers.

Radishes can actually be a companion plant to other vegetables. They grow well with peas, lettuce, and cucumbers. Plant chervil (*Anthriscus cerefolium*) near radishes if you want to improve their growth and flavor. The radishes will also improve the growth and taste of chervil. If you want to protect your radishes from pests, plant nasturtium (*Tropaeolum spp.*). It deters beetles, aphids, whiteflies, and other pests. Do not plant hyssop (*Hyssopus officinalis*) near radishes.

Squash is another favorite plant in the vegetable garden. If you want to repel squash bugs, plant nasturtiums (*Tropaeolum spp.*) or tansy (*Tanacetum vulgare*) near the squash. Squash and any other plants in the squash family are good for other reasons. Their leaves can provide green mulch in your garden. With their low growth, more water is retained in the soil.

Borage (*Borago officinalis*) is a great companion plant for strawberries because it attracts honeybees, as well as strengthens resistance to insects and disease. Do not plant tansy (*Tanacetum vulgare*) near strawberries, however, and don't plant strawberries near cabbage.

Just one little note: Keep fennel (*Foeniculum vulgare, F. vulgare dulce*) by itself. It's very valuable to the garden, because it attracts beneficial wasps and insects. However, most plants, especially beans and tomatoes, do not like it.

These are just some examples for your vegetable garden. A listing below provides more information on companion plants that you may want to use in your garden.

There are so many rewards when you grow your garden: You can find a sanctuary around your home that relaxes and invigorates you. You can eat better food by growing your own vegetables. You can attract butterflies, hummingbirds, and other living creatures to your private space. Through companion planting you do more than just create a space of beauty. You help sustain and add something back to the Earth. You create a place of diversity, which maintains the balance that is needed in life.

Companion Herbs for the Garden

Allium Family

Allium is a good companion plant for cabbage, raspberries, grapevines, and roses. It repels mice, Japanese beetles, aphids, and peach borers. It also attracts beneficial insects.

Anise

Anise (*Pimpinella anisum*) repels aphids and fleas, but it is not a good companion plant for carrots.

Angelica

Angelica (*Angelica archangelica* in Europe, *A. atropurpurea* in the United States, and *A. sinensis* in China) is often called a trap plant, because it attracts aphids. It is also called a beneficial plant, because it attracts parasitic wasps, lady beetles, lacewings, and other beneficial insects. Do not plant it near carrots. Also be aware that the fresh roots of angelica are poisonous. Angelica also looks very similar to water hemlock (*Cicuta maculate*), which is an extremely poisonous plant.

Basil

Basil (*Ocimum basilicum*) improves the taste of tomatoes. It repels mosquitoes as well as flies, but it does not do well near rue.

Borage

Borage (*Borage officinalis*) is a good companion plant for squash, strawberries, and tomatoes. It deters the tomato hornworm, and it attracts honey bees.

Caraway

Caraway (*Carum curvi*) , with its deep taproot, loosens the soil and also pulls up nutrients from the subsoil.

Catnip

Catnip (*Nepeta cataria*) is a good overall companion plant because of the number of insects it can repel. However, it can also repel beneficial insects. It repels the cabbage moth. It is invasive, so consider planting it in a pot rather than directly into the soil. It attracts cats, which may prevent moles and voles.

Chamomile

Chamomile (*Charmaemelum nobile*) improves the flavor of cabbage and onions. Do not plant near carrots.

Chervil

Chervil (*Anthriscus cerefolium*) is a good companion plant for radishes because it improves their vigor and flavor. Radishes also improve the vigor and flavor of chervil.

Coriander/Cilantro

Corriander/cilantro (*Coriandrum sativum*) is a good overall companion plant because it repels aphids. However, do not plant it near fennel.

Dill

Dill (*Anethum graveolens*) improves its vigor and flavor of cabbage and attracts beneficial insects. However, do not plant it near carrots; it can stunt their growth. Although it is a good trap plant for the tomato hornworm, planting it too close to tomatoes may reduce their growth.

Fennel

Fennel (*Foeniculum vulgare*) should be planted away from most plants, especially beans and tomatoes.

Garlic

Garlic (*Allium sativum*) will repel aphids and Japanese beetles when planted near roses. It improves the taste of cabbage. Garlic is also said to prevent some fungal infections. Do not plant near peas or beans.

Hyssop

Hyssop (*Hyssopus officinalis*) is a good companion to the cabbage family because it attracts cabbage moths. It is also a good companion plant for grapes, but do not plant it near radishes.

Lavender

Lavender (*Lavandula spp.*) is a good overall companion plant because it deters a number of insects. It will also deter slugs and snails when planted around the border of gardens.

Lovage

Lovage (*Levisticum officinale*) is a good all-around companion plant. It improves the vigor of most plants and the flavor of vegetables, and it increases the vigor of bush and pole beans.

Marjoram

Marjoram (*Origanum majorana*) is an excellent overall companion plant. It improves the vigor of all plants and the overall flavor of vegetables.

Mint

Mint (*Mentha spp.*) is a good companion plant for cabbage since it deters the white cabbage moth and improves its vigor. It is also a good companion plant for tomatoes since it improves the vigor of tomatoes. Peppermint and spearmint are especially good repellents of ants, aphids, flea beetles, and cabbage moth.

Oregano

Oregano (*Origamum spp.*) is an excellent overall companion plant because it deters many insects. Be careful when purchasing oregano to verify the botanical name. Some marjoram is also called oregano.

Parsley

Parsley (*Petroselinum crispum*; *P. hortense*; *P. sativum*) is a good companion plant for roses, asparagus, corn, and tomatoes.

Pennyroyal

Pennyroyal (*Mentha pulegium* in Europe and *Hedeama pulegioides* in the United States) is a good overall companion plant because it deter ants.

Rosemary

Rosemary (*Rosmarinus officinalis*) is an excellent overall companion plant as it can deter snails and slugs when branches are laid on the ground in the garden. It is a good companion plant for cabbage because it deters the cabbage moth. It is a good companion plant for beans because it deters bean beetles. It is a good companion plant for carrots since it deters carrot flies. It is a good companion plant for sage.

Rue

Rue (*Ruta graveolens*) is a good companion plant for roses and raspberries since it deters Japanese beetles. However, do not plant it near sweet basil, sage, or cabbage.

Sage

Sage (*Salvis officinalis*) is a good companion plant for cabbage as it deters the cabbage worm. Good companion plant for carrots as it deters the carrot fly. It is also a good companion plant for marjoram, rosemary, strawberries, and tomatoes. Do not plant it near cucumbers, rue, or carrots.

Tansy

Tansy (*Tanacetum vulgare*) is a good overall companion plant because it deters ants. It is especially a good companion plant for cabbage since it deters cabbage worms and cutworms. It also improves the vigor of roses and the flavor of raspberries. However, do not plant it near tomatoes or pole beans.

Tarragon

Tarragon (*Artemisia dracunculus*) is good throughout the garden because it deters a number of pests.

Thyme

Thyme (*Thymus vulgaris, T. serphyllum*) is a good overall companion plant, but it is especially good for cabbage since it deters the cabbage loopers and cabbage worms. It will deter slugs and snails when planted around the border of gardens. It also attracts beneficial insects.

How To Contain Your Garden

☙ by Alice DeVille ❧

After winter's icy blast sub-
sides and the soil thaws,
the great outdoors awakens
to the warmth of the sun and the
spring rains. Every little seed, bulb,
or plant hibernating beneath the soil
gets ready for its seasonal debut.
Deciduous trees and shrubs develop
new foliage and blossoms, while
perennial plants and flowers push
their way through the soil to accent
the landscape. And our decks, patios,
and empty window boxes patiently
wait for a touch of TLC.

In the meantime, gardening catalogs arrive in the mail. Online vendors
try to tempt you with preseason sales
touting the effectiveness of foolproof
supplies that guarantee you a bumper

crop of vegetables or a dazzling array of dahlias. Not to be outdone, local nurseries send flyers announcing weekly plant specials and the desirability of using their diverse soil amendments to produce the best garden results in town. The Law of Attraction is at work! What else is the passionate gardener to do but get in touch with her itchy green thumb?

While every piece of your outdoor space deserves the opportunity to sparkle with plant life, this article focuses on effective techniques for using container gardening to grow your flowers, fruits, herbs, and vegetables. Whether you use the space on decks and patios, or parcel off a small amount of your backyard to install a raised bed, you'll find tips for making your gardening project a rewarding experience. So slather on the sunscreen, grab sunglasses and sunhat, and dig in. Let the garden games begin!

Before You Plant

Using pencil and paper, draw a plan for your gardening project. If you are placing containers on your deck, evaluate the location of the sun, shade, and wind conditions. Some decks sit high off the ground and get bombarded with gusty winds; others nestle in trees and get very little sun, which provides ideal conditions for shade-loving plants and flowers rather than vegetables. But if you are blessed to have a sunny patio or deck, you have the perfect space for growing most herbs, vegetables, and annuals. Capitalize on limited space by arranging plants in layers—some directly on the floor, others in hanging baskets, some on tiered plant stands and others on railings. Window boxes or balconies are also ideal for growing bushy or trailing plants.

If you prefer to cultivate a variety of herbs and vegetables in a plot, consider the merits of building a three-foot-square or four-foot-square raised bed. They work particularly well if your regional soil is too hard and rocky for growing plants. Instead of struggling to change these undesirable growing conditions, plant your garden over the top of the poor terrain. Combine the required amounts of topsoil, garden soil, and organic compost within the bed frame (wood or synthetic) and you're ready to plant.

If you plan to use old containers, however, you should clean out any remaining soil and start with fresh planting materials. Your yard probably has spots that could use the addition of the leftover enriched soil, especially around the house foundation or in sparse or eroding areas. You can omit this step if perennials were planted in the containers.

If you need to buy containers, the crop, herb, or flower you want to plant determines which planters to purchase. Allow enough space (width, height, and volume) or your plant will fail. Gardeners make the most of very limited space by selecting containers suitable for the job. Walk around your garden center to examine the variety of shapes, sizes, and materials of containers. Consider how attractively they will display your plants, and go for color and texture to accentuate the beauty of your harvest. Vary the shapes—round, square, oblong, or over-the-fence style planting buckets are available.

While many gardeners mount wood boxes on their windows or decks, manufacturers also offer beautiful handcrafted, copper-finished stainless steel boxes that are as beautiful as your blooms. Tall planters that are columnar in shape can grace the corners of patios with lush green foliage and graceful blossoms. Consider using whiskey barrel planters with the look of weathered wood to house lush displays of seasonal bloomers. These giant planters often grace the end of driveways where their gorgeous blooms welcome visitors. Many whiskey barrels come with self-watering features and contain a large reservoir for water so the plants never suffer from drought.

Drainage, Pots, and Soils

Be sure you invest in outdoor pots that you supplement with good drainage material, but you may have to put drainage holes in the bottom of containers that don't have them. Without good drainage, plant roots rot and your plant will die. Some planters come with wheels, especially larger ones that are too heavy to move. These containers work well with tomatoes, squash, cucumbers, beans, peas, potatoes, and melons that need space to branch out. A single plant can yield a bumper crop of delicious veggies. Last year, I had a cherry tomato plant that yielded a steady output of tomatoes from July to November when the last of the red tomatoes froze on the vines.

Purchase planters that are 16 to 24 inches wide for these crops. Most other flower or vegetable plants and herbs need pots that are 10 to 14 inches wide; smaller ones are best for indoor use, transplants, or small specimens. Raised bed containers that you assemble yourself work well on your deck or patio, providing an abundance of growing space. They come in a variety of sizes. Some hold over 200 quarts of soil and have a depth of 18 inches, making them perfect for cultivating hardy vegetable plants.

Some enthusiasts use "grow bags" made with breathable

components to plant herbs and vegetables. These bags also come in varying sizes that hold 20 to 75 quarts of planting soil. The advantage of these bags is at season's end, you can empty the soil from the bags, clean them, and fold them neatly for easy storage and use in the next season. By using large containers, you get more bang for your buck because of the variety of plants they can hold. I once saw Martha Stewart and a guest on her TV show take a 20-inch-wide round planter and put plants in four corners with a tomato plant in the middle. Her "corner" choices were broccoli, squash, peas, and cucumber. When I tried it, the container got very crowded in no time at all, so I recommend using only three plants to a pot of this size. Every one of these plants needs room to spread out; the peas need a stake so their vines climb up the pole like tomato plants. Often, gardeners place trellises against a wall or deck rail and grow their bean, pea, and tomato plants next to the trellises so that their vines climb easily and establish themselves firmly in this type of setting.

Beautiful Flower Boxes

You can really go to town creating gorgeous floral displays for your deck, patio, or window. Go nostalgic by filling your window box with heirloom flowers like bleeding heart, with its long, dangling, crimson red hearts that form colorful streamers, or the fragrant vining sweet peas that come in shades of pink, white, purple, and red.

Annuals that work particularly well in containers include begonias, coleus, geraniums, impatiens, marigolds, nasturtiums, pansies, and petunias. Clusters of variegated coleus or plump, showy petunias beautifully accent your home's exterior, lending an air of elegance to your windows and balconies.

Celosia and dwarf snapdragons look striking in a variety of containers. Marigolds keep pests away from vegetables so you can add them to vegetable containers or place them right next to your tomato and squash plants. The tall variety of marigold works best in a raised bed garden while the smaller type thrives in deck planters or window boxes. If you grow them from seeds, be sure you thin them out and transplant them or they will quickly become pot-bound.

Hanging Baskets and Deck Rail Planters

Although I plant many of these species, one of my personal favorites for a hanging basket is the gerbera daisy. They tolerate full sun and come in a variety of hues. Gerberas also do well in "saddle planters," a type of self-mounting planter that fits snugly on your deck, balcony, or porch rail without needing installation tools. Planting two or three shades of gerbera makes a showy statement. Try filling a hanging basket with fuchsia and place it on a tree branch where it blooms all season—these flowers need some shade. Geraniums, petunias, and pansies positively radiate in hanging baskets. Purchase the self-watering type baskets and your flowers will thrive while you reduce some of your watering time. Avoid buying hanging baskets with inexpensive plastic or flimsy stiff plant hangers—a heavy wind will snap them off and ruin your floral display. You can salvage those broken planters by replacing the hangers with solid steel hangers that fit perfectly around rimmed pots, or use the woven type rope hangers, which are much sturdier and can be used on rimmed or rimless pots indoors or out. Be sure you know which flowers tolerate sun and which need some shade; otherwise your lovely blooms will shrivel up and wilt quickly. Deadhead leggy blooms and dried blossoms to encourage flower growth all season. Many flower growers recommend adding a thin layer of mulch to containers to help retain moisture. If you plant seeds, don't put any mulch in the container until the specimen has grown a few inches or you may kill the seedlings.

The Perfect Soil

To aid your success in yielding beautiful container blooms, use lightweight, airy soil specifically made for containers. Some varieties incorporate harvested sphagnum peat, perlite, and vermiculite to help retain moisture without clumping or getting heavy. A number of soil suppliers also offer a standard soil for self-watering containers that allows the mix to act as a wick, carrying water from the planter's reservoir to the root system. This soil may also include limestone, so you won't have to buy separate bags to mix into your container. Mixes come in both organic and standard compositions; you will pay more for the organic variety, as well as for those mixes that have added pre-measured soil amendments. Avoid using top-soil in your containers—it is way too heavy and the roots can't breathe. Annuals need balanced plant food and a slow-release fertilizer. Before adding soil to an empty container, be sure to add a layer of natural stones so that when you water the plant, water doesn't rush right through the soil and out of the container. A mistake that new gardeners often make is to skimp on the depth of the soil; if you don't fill the container with enough soil, your plants will have shallow roots and skimpy top growth.

Perennials stay rooted in your planter for years, unlike the annual and the vegetable crops. Annuals can handle time-released or organic fertilizers and do well with aged compost —look for the odor-free variety and your nose will thank you.

Note: You don't need to fertilize for the first few weeks or months after planting if you have used soil that includes fertilizer. Each time you water, some of the nutrients leach out and the plants will have to be fed to remain healthy and vibrant. If you have specimens with pale color that look like they aren't putting out new growth, they probably need food. Water plants daily when excessively hot weather persists.

Selecting and Potting Your Plants

When you visit the nursery to select plants, seeds, and containers, purchase the planting soils you will need to maximize the quality of your gardening efforts. Given the space requirements that vegetables need to yield succulent growth, you will increase your chances of success by following these general guidelines:

Read planting directions for every vegetable purchase; if the plants don't include tags with specific information, speak to an on-site expert. Most garden centers have an information station where the pros assist customers with questions and recommend purchases.

Select specific soil blends for vegetable and herb planting (fruits, too, if you have made them a part of your design). Look for usage information on every bag of soil before you load it into your cart. Some bags have similar coloring and design and you can easily mistake one for the other. Certain bagged soils contain toxins and cannot be used to plant vegetables. Read the information on the bag carefully to avoid later problems. Most soils that specify they are safe for flower and vegetable use may need amendments based on what you grow.

Keep a notebook that includes details like what, where, and

when you purchased and planted your selections. If you don't leave the little plant markers in the soil where you have installed the plant, put them in your notebook in an envelope or tape them to the page where you have listed the planting details. Allow enough room to include information about when you fertilize and feed the plants. Note any problems and how you treated the problem. Take pictures of your plants and flowers periodically so you have an additional record of their progress. You can also scan your notes and store them on your computer for future use.

Seeds go a long way and will keep reproducing an abundant crop. Be sure not to place too many seeds in one spot. Plant more than one variety of lettuce seeds in long saddle boxes or raised beds for best results. Leaf lettuce works best unless you use a six-foot or longer raised bed and can actually plant head lettuce. Seed tapes are a foolproof way to plant where space really counts. These tapes are strips of biodegradable paper that are embedded with perfectly spaced seeds that you simply roll into a prepared furrow and cover with more soil. Your planting is more precise and you'll have to do very little thinning. The most common seed tape vegetables are chard, radish, spring onion, carrot, lettuce, and beet strips. Be on the lookout for weeds, grass shoots, and different species of plants among your sprouting seedlings. You will notice them once the plants start maturing, and they will have to go.

Plants need containers that are large, wide, and deep when planting potatoes, onions, radishes, tomatoes, eggplant, squash, cucumbers, cabbage, beans, peas, melons, broccoli, and peppers. Although you can plant them from seed, the easiest method is to buy young plants and put them in the soil when the danger of frost has passed in your climate zone. Tomatoes and onions need at least 12 hours of sunlight. A single potato plant yields approximately 12 to 14 pounds of potatoes. Adding a small marigold plant to your pots helps keep critters at bay. The shallow roots of strawberries, raspberries, and blueberries make them ideal container growers. If you use your outdoor patio or deck frequently, don't plant your fruit there or the birds will enjoy it right along with you. Surround your plants with bird netting to keep them and other animals away.

Watch Your Garden Grow

Container gardening in your own private spaces allows for unlimited creative expression. Few things in life offer more payback than your personal gardening success. For an incomparable feeling, explore the wonder of helping things grow. The beauty and the bounty are yours to enjoy.

Culinary
Herbs

Grilling with Herbs

≈ by Susan Pesznecker ≈

Herbs can turn a barbecued meal into something magnificent! Whether you brine, rub, infuse, baste, stuff, or sprinkle, using herbs in your next grilled meal is guaranteed to bring rave reviews. Using herbs when you barbecue is a fun and inexpensive way to experiment with your inner chef. For best results, use only the freshest ingredients. Chop your own garlic, grate your own lemon peel, and grind your own black pepper, and you'll taste the difference.

In culinary terms, barbecuing refers to cooking foods over low, slow heat, while grilling refers to quick cooking over a higher heat. Barbecuing or grilling over direct heat means putting the food directly above the coals. Using indirect heat means that half of the grill space holds hot coals with the food arranged on the opposite side of the grill, allowing gentler cooking.

When judging heat: "low heat" means you can hold your hand over the coals for quite a while before you have to pull it away; "moderate heat" means you might last 4 or 5 seconds; and "high heat" means 2 to 3 seconds or less.

Brines

In a brine, food is immersed in a sweetened, salted, flavored liquid bath. Brining tenderizes food and makes it juicy and flavorful. It also adds salt; keep this in mind for diners on low-salt diets.

When brining, use enough liquid to fully submerge the food. Brine time varies according to the size and nature of the food item: a few pieces of shrimp might be brined for 30 minutes, while a turkey might need a couple of days. Keep food refrigerated while it's brining. Rinse the food thoroughly before cooking.

Key Recipe #1 / Cold Brine

Stir ½ to ¾ cup salt into 1 gallon of water. Add other ingredients as desired. Hold at room temperature overnight, then use.

Key Recipe #2 / Hot Brine

Combine ¾ cup salt and ¾ cup sugar in 1 gallon of water. Add other ingredients as desired. Bring to a boil, cool to room temperature, and use immediately.

For best results, use kosher salt. For "sugar," use white, raw (turbinado), or brown sugar, or try maple syrup or molasses. Create interesting effects with apple cider, fruit juice, vinegar, and alcohol, being careful not to create too much acidity in the mixture. Experiment with garlic, onions, citrus fruits, pepper, herbs, and spices.

Brine for Pork (Use Key Recipe #2)

Substitute apple cider for half the water and use brown sugar. Add one sliced onion, 2 tablespoons dry mustard, 2 tablespoons chopped garlic, 3 or 4 bay leaves, and ½ cup bourbon (optional). Brine 4 to 8 hours.

Brine for Chicken or Turkey (Use Key Recipe #2)

Add ¾ cup soy sauce, ½ cup apple cider vinegar, 3 to 4 tablespoons chopped garlic, 3 tablespoons fresh-ground black pepper, 2 tablespoons ground ginger, and 1 tablespoon ground allspice. Brine 24 to 48 hours.

Marinades

A marinade uses a combination of wet and dry ingredients to thoroughly moisten and flavor the food. Some marinades also tenderize the food or change its color: ceviche, which uses citrus to "cook" (actually to change the opacity and texture) seafood by marinating, is an example.

Common marinade ingredients include oil, sugar, salt, soy sauce, vinegar, herbs, and spices. The marinade is applied to all surfaces of the food; the food is then tucked into the refrigerator for one or more hours. Marinade may or may not be rinsed off before the food is cooked.

Sweet-soy Steak Marinade

Combine 2 tablespoons vegetable oil, 1 tablespoon sesame oil, 2 tablespoons rice wine vinegar, ¼ cup soy sauce, 1 tablespoons chopped garlic, 1 tablespoon grated fresh ginger, 4 chopped scallions, and 2 tablespoons dark brown sugar. Place in a large self-sealing bag with a flank or flat iron steak. Marinate for 4 to 24 hours. Grill over high heat and slice in thin strips to serve.

Herbal Chicken Marinade

Combine 1 teaspoon chopped garlic, 1 teaspoon chopped rosemary, 1 teaspoon thyme, and 1 teaspoon lemon juice. Add olive oil to form a thick paste. Pat onto the chicken pieces and marinate for 1 or more hours. Grill over indirect heat.

Dry Rubs

A rub works like a marinade except that it uses only dry ingredients and oils to flavor the food. Some rubs also tenderize, impart color, or change the texture of the food.

Common rub ingredients include sugar, salt, and various herbs and seasonings. The rub is patted onto to all surfaces of the food; the food is then refrigerated for 1 to 8 hours. Rubs may or may not be rinsed off before the food is cooked.

Dry Rub "Curry Cure" for Salmon

Combine 2 tablespoons sugar, 1 tablespoon salt, 1 tablespoon curry powder, and 1 tablespoon dry mustard. Sprinkle over the fish side of a 1- to 3-pound salmon filet. Cover and chill for 1 to 3 hours. Rinse the salmon thoroughly before cooking; the color will have deepened and the flavor will be lusciously accented.

Dry Rub for Pork Ribs

Sprinkle the ribs (both sides; remove the silver skin underlying the ribs) with salt, black pepper, red pepper flakes, garlic powder, crushed anise seed, onion powder, hickory smoked salt, allspice, ginger, brown sugar, and dry mustard. Leave rub on for 2 to 12 hours; do not remove before grilling.

Stuffings

Using a stuffing is a fabulous way to add flavor and moisture to a food from the inside out. Stuffings use a "base" of ingredients—often bread, but sometimes fruits, grains, seeds, vegetables, etc.—with herbs and other ingredients as well.

Key Recipe #3 / Poultry Stuffing

Cook ¼ cup diced onion and ½ cup diced celery in 4 tablespoons butter until softened. Stir in 4 cups bread cubes, torn biscuits, or corn bread. Add ½ teaspoon salt, ¼ teaspoon black pepper, ½ teaspoon sage, ½ teaspoon thyme, ¼ teaspoon marjoram, and a pinch of allspice. Add enough hot chicken stock so the mixture is damp, but not wet. This stuffs a large chicken or small turkey.

Key Recipe #4 / Fish Stuffing

Stuff a whole, cleaned fish with slices of lemon and fresh, chopped marjoram, tarragon, or thyme (adjust amount to your own preference). Add a few slices of onion and some fresh parsley. Grill over moderate heat, 2 to 3 minutes per side.

Stuffed Salmon

Stuff a whole salmon—or a section—with equal parts chopped apple, celery, and carrot. Moisten with soy sauce, add a number of thin lemon slices, and then sprinkle with chopped thyme. Lay the salmon on a large piece of chicken wire. (The chicken wire should be large enough to also fold over the top of the salmon.) Enclose the stuffed fish "taco style" with the wire, and fold the edges together to secure the salmon inside. Grill over indirect heat for about 20 minutes, turning once. Check for doneness. When the chicken wire is undone, the skin adheres to it, leaving the fish ready to serve. Top with Otto's salmon sauce (page 82). This preparation method works with any large, whole fish.

Bastes

Basting means brushing food with liquid as it cooks. Bastes add richness, oiliness, sweetness, or flavor to the outside surfaces of the food but don't penetrate the food. A bunch of herbs—tied with kitchen twine—makes a quick basting brush and adds flavor, too.

Bastes typically include melted butter or oil, various herbs and flavorings, and sometimes alcohol. Baste the food every 10 to 15 minutes as it cooks, particularly during the last half of cooking. Reserve sweetened bastes for the last half hour of cooking as they tend to scorch.

Key Recipe #5 / Herb-Butter Baste

Combine unsalted melted butter with black pepper and chopped fresh herbs.

Quick and Easy Barbecue Baste

Combine 2 parts bottled barbecue sauce, 1 part dry sherry, and 2 tablespoons of mixed fresh herbs (chopped thyme, lemon balm, garlic, and parsley are excellent).

Eastern Vegetable Baste

Mix ½ cup yogurt, 1 teaspoon lemon peel, and fresh or dried dill. Adjust seasonings to your own taste. Thin with olive oil.

Sweet Peanut Sauce and Baste

Blend ½ cup peanut butter, 1 tablespoon tamari, a dash of chili sauce, a handful of fresh basil (chopped), several mint leaves (chopped), and a pinch of allspice. Thin with warm water or coconut milk. This is excellent on fruit, chicken, and pork; it's also a fabulous finishing sauce (below).

Shakes

A shake is a dry seasoning mixture applied to the food as it cooks. Most shakes include salt, pepper, and a number of herbs of other flavoring agents (e.g., citrus peel). Shakes add one more layer of flavor to your food; they're particularly delicious when combined with a baste or sprinkled as food comes off the grill.

Key Recipe #6 / All-Purpose Shake

Combine 1 teaspoon salt, ½ teaspoon pepper, ½ teaspoon garlic powder, ½ teaspoon onion powder, and ¼ teaspoon paprika.

Hamburger Shake

Combine 1 teaspoon salt, ½ teaspoon pepper, ½ teaspoon garlic powder, ½ teaspoon onion powder, ¼ teaspoon red pepper flakes, and ¼ teaspoon hickory smoked salt.

Chicken Shake

Combine 1 teaspoon salt, ½ teaspoon pepper, ¼ teaspoon garlic powder, ¼ teaspoon paprika, and ¼ teaspoon poultry seasoning.

Butter

A compound butter is softened butter to which herbs and flavorings have been added. The butter is formed into a log and chilled; slices of the compound butter are placed atop hot food as it comes off the grill, adding a rich finish.

Key Recipe #7 / Compound Butter

Combine 1 softened stick of unsalted butter with finely chopped fresh herbs. Use 2 tablespoons chives, 1 tablespoon rosemary, 1 tablespoon sage, and 1 tablespoon thyme (adjust amounts to suit your taste). Adding 1 tablespoon olive oil makes this even more elegant.

Finishing Sauces

A finishing sauce is a refined sauce served with food. Use a finishing sauce to accent flavors incorporated earlier—through marinades, bastes, shakes, etc.—or to introduce a new taste.

Otto's Salmon Sauce

Combine ½ pound butter (2 sticks), 1 minced clove garlic, 4 tablespoons soy sauce, 2 tablespoons prepared mustard, 4 tablespoons ketchup, 1 teaspoon horseradish, and the juice of ½ lemon. Stir in a small saucepan over low heat until blended. Don't overheat or the ingredients will separate; if this happens, beat with a whisk or immersion blender to recombine.

Lemon Butter Sauce

Char lemon halves over direct heat with cut side down. Squeeze the juice into melted butter for a wonderful seafood or vegetable dip.

Flambés

Do you have a flare for showmanship? A flambé might be just what you're looking for. Pour herb or citrus-infused alcohol over the food and ignite. It will burn briefly with spectacular effect. Do not do this with food on the grill as a dangerous flare-up could result! Flambé is wonderful with sugared grilled fruit; serve over vanilla ice cream.

Herbs for Grilled Meats and Poultry

Herbs for meats include black pepper, cumin, garlic, mustard, orange, red pepper flakes, rosemary, and sage.

Herbs for fowl include allspice, bay, garlic, ginger, lemon, marjoram, orange, sage, and thyme.

Middle Eastern Lamb

Create a marinade of unflavored yogurt, mint, lemon peel and juice, coriander, a pinch of cumin, and grated cardamom. Marinate lamb chops in the mixture for 2 to 4 hours, reserving some of the marinade. Grill quickly over moderate-high direct heat, brushing again with the reserved mixture. Shake black pepper and more lemon peel over the finished meat.

Open Sesame Pork

Brine a pork tenderloin. Cut into ½-inch-thick slices. Make a baste of equal parts sesame seeds, minced garlic, and chili-sesame oil. Thin with soy sauce or tamari. Grill the pork slices quickly over high direct heat, 1 to 2 minutes per side. Baste with the sesame mixture while cooking.

Herbs for Grilled Fish

Herbs for fish include chives, fennel, garlic, lemon, marjoram, parsley, and thyme.

Grilled Fish Steak

Grill sturdy fish steaks (e.g., sturgeon, halibut, bass) over moderate heat until barely done. Finish with a sauce of melted butter with crushed fennel seed, dill, thyme, marjoram, capers, or whatever other spices sound tasty.

Grilled Shrimp

Rub brined shrimp with olive oil and dry rub with your choice of black pepper, cumin, chili powder, parsley, paprika, and savory. Cook very quickly—no more than a couple of minutes per side—and finish with a lemon-parsley compound butter. Serve over angel hair pasta.

Herbs for Grilled Vegetables

Good herbs for vegetables include chives, cilantro, dill, fennel, garlic, lemon, parsley, rosemary, summer savory, and thyme.

Key Recipe #8 / Grilled Vegetables

Slice vegetables ½-inch thick* (see note below). Brush with olive oil and sprinkle with salt, pepper, and herbs of choice. Grill over moderate heat for a few minutes, turning until you see grill marks and the veggies are becoming tender and savory. Good choices for this: fennel, summer squash, eggplant, and heirloom tomatoes.

Note: Parboil tough or fibrous veggies (e.g., carrots, jicama, parsnips) until barely tender. Plunge into ice water to stop the cooking, and then proceed with grilling.

Soak corn—in its husks—in ice water for 2 to 3 hours. Drain, then grill over moderate heat until the husks are charred. Serve with a mixture of ½ cup mayonnaise, 1 minced garlic clove, 1 tablespoon chopped fresh parsley, ¼ teaspoon black pepper, and ½ teaspoon summer savory.

Char sweet peppers or tomatillos over moderate direct heat until skin blackens and blisters. Dress with olive oil, balsamic vinegar, lemon, garlic, capers, and a sprinkling of *herbs de Provence* (a mixture of savory, fennel, basil, thyme, and lavender).

Spice-rubbed Veggies

Peel carrots, parsnips, beets, etc. Combine 1 tablespoon each of salt and brown sugar, 1 teaspoon cumin, ½ teaspoon black pepper, ¼ teaspoon fresh nutmeg, and a pinch of cinnamon. Roll the veggies in the mixture; grill over indirect heat until tender.

Mint-onion Relish

Thinly slice fresh sweet onion. Toss with seasoned rice wine vinegar and vegetable oil. Stir in 1 to 2 tablespoon of chopped fresh mint. This goes well with fish or vegetables.

Grilled Fennel Salad

Grill thick slices of fennel, prepared as in Key Recipe #8. Cut oranges in half and grill with the cut side down. Serve the fennel on a bed of mixed greens and squeeze the grilled oranges over the top. Options: Top with blue cheese and/or crumbled bacon.

Herbed Potatoes

Slice peeled potatoes ½-inch thick onto a square of foil. Add olive oil, chopped fresh chives, fresh thyme, and black pepper.

Top with 1 tablespoon water. Close the foil tightly and place on the grill over moderate heat. Test after 15 minutes. For sweet potatoes, use butter instead of olive oil and top with brown sugar, fresh nutmeg, and black pepper.

Herbs for Grilled Fruits and Desserts

Best herbs for fruits include cinnamon, lavender, lemon, lime, mint, and nutmeg.

Key Recipe #9 / Grilled Fruit

Slice fruits ½-inch thick. Brush with neutral vegetable oil and sprinkle with turbinado sugar (or honey), lemon or lime juice, and herbs of choice. Grill over low to moderate heat for a few minutes, turning every so often until the pieces become tender and savory. Good choices for this include: stone fruits (peaches, plums, apples, etc.), mango, and pineapple.

Key Recipe #10 / Foil-cooked Fruit

Slice apples or pears ½-inch thick onto a large square of foil. Sprinkle with sugar or honey and your choice of cinnamon, nutmeg, lemon peel, or allspice. Add 1 tablespoon water. Set over an indirect moderate fire for 20 minutes, turning occasionally. Open packet and test for doneness.

Special Effects

Grilled Herbal Pizza

Grill pre-made pizza shells or flatbread over indirect heat. Top with sauce, cheese, and a handful of fresh chopped herbs and veggies. Finish with a spice shake.

Grilled Tofu

Brush firm tofu with sesame oil and season to taste with salt, pepper, minced garlic, and herbs of choice. Create a mixture of juice from 1 lemon, 1 tablespoon of olive oil, and ¼ teaspoon of tahini. Adjust seasoning to your own taste. Grill over moderate heat until crispy, basting near the end with the lemon mixture.

Use sturdy rosemary branches as skewers—they're functional and add flavor.

"Smoke" Your Food with Herbs

Soak a handful of fresh herbs in water for two or more hours. Shake dry and cut into small pieces. Toss a few at a time—still damp—onto hot coals to flavor your foods with herbal smoke.

Have fun adding herbs to your usual cooking techniques— a world of flavor awaits you at the grill!

Go Wild: Free-Range & Game Meat Seasonings

⫷ by Elizabeth Barrette ⫸

An important key to cooking is the combination of flavors that enhance each other. To do justice to a particular cut of meat, you must understand its characteristics and know what herbs, spices, and vegetables or fruit will bring out the best in it. Wild game and free-range livestock produce meat tastes rather different from the commercially raised meat that most people are used to eating. Therefore, these meats benefit from a somewhat different selection of seasonings.

Wild meat comes from undomesticated animals that roam through the fields and woods eating whatever they can find. Free-range is a term used for domestic animals that are not fed on grains or commercial chow, but rather are put out to pasture to graze, browse, or otherwise forage for themselves. Grass-fed is a similar term.

Wild game includes any undomesticated animals that are hunted or trapped instead of farm-raised. Some game animals are allowed on free-range farms, including bison and deer. Large game animals include elk, bison, and deer. Small game includes rabbits, hares, raccoons, and squirrels. Fowl include pheasants and wild turkeys, ducks, and geese. Many types of fish are also caught wild, such as salmon, trout, crappie, bass, and bluegill.

Livestock raised on a free-range or grass-fed basis has access to pasture, which gives the meat a more robust flavor and texture. Red meats are usually described as grass-fed, particularly beef, goat, and lamb but sometimes pork—pigs can be ranged in a forest. Poultry include chickens plus domestic turkeys, ducks, and geese; they are usually described as free-range. Animal products other than meats include eggs, milk, butter, and cheese; these may be tagged with a variety of descriptions.

In all cases, the types of plants eaten by these animals contribute to the flavor of the meat (or milk, eggs, and other products) they produce. Because they get more exercise than confined animals, their muscles are more developed, which typically gives the meat a deeper color and more flavor. This also tends to reduce the amount of fat in the meat, because that exercise also burns calories. Animals that are allowed to forage for food don't get flabby as confined animals do.

This means two things for a cook. First, the richer and more complex flavor gives you more to work with in harmonizing seasonings; and second, the lower fat changes how the meat behaves when heated, so you have to work with that or else add some cooking fat.

Herbs for Wild and Free-Range Foods

Some general principles apply in selecting the seasonings for wild and free-range meats. First, some meats can support a stronger range of flavorings than domestic meats without being drowned out. Consider spices with hot, sharp, or resinous flavors. Second, some (such as fish) have very subtle flavors that respond best to delicate herbs. Third, everything is affected by the forage, so pay attention to leafy green notes; all the better if you can use herbs that grow in the same area. Also bear in mind that wild goes well with wild. If you're serving wild game or free-range meat, consider using wild mushrooms, wild rice, wild onions, or foraged salad greens in your side dishes. Currants, lingonberries, blackberries, or spiced crabapples can add a tart or sweet touch to the meal.

Asafoetida

Asafoetida (*Ferula asafoetida*) may be used as a vegetable, but powder made from the plant is more often used in cooking. Asafoetida powder has a pungent, sharp, musky odor. A pinch or two brings out robust and bitter notes in a recipe, preventing flavors from becoming bland or insipid—especially useful when cooking meat in a yogurt or cream sauce. It has antispasmodic, carminative, and digestive qualities and goes well with grass-fed lamb and other dark, robust meats.

Caraway

Caraway (*Carum carvi*): This biennial herb has feathery leaves and small white flowers yielding edible seeds. Seeds have a sharp aromatic flavor. Caraway has carminative and warming qualities, and also prevents bad breath. Used in bread, it makes an excellent side dish; it also flavors sausages, meatballs, and other spiced meat blends.

Cayenne

Cayenne (*Capsicum annuum*) is a short bushy plant that produces peppers which are typically dried and sold as powder. The pepper can be moderately to intensely hot. It has cleansing, digestive, stimulating, and warming qualities. Add a pinch or two to casseroles or other mixed dishes for a subtle warmth, or a little more for a high, bright note. It is an excellent base for spicy sauces or gravies and for herbal rubs on robust meats, such as beef, lamb, goat, venison, or elk.

Cranberry

Cranberries (*Vaccinium macrocarpon*) grow on woody bushes in wetlands produce bright red berries. Cranberry juice, dried cranberries, and sauces are all popular. Use cranberry juice in stews or crock pots, or as a base for marinades. Dried cranberries are good in fruit/nut stuffings for rolled venison or elk roasts. Cranberry sauce makes an excellent accompaniment for dark meats, such as turkey, duck, goose, or elk.

Dill

Dill (*Anethum graveolens*) produces tall stalks with thread-like leaves and tiny yellow flowers followed by narrow seeds. Dill weed (dried or fresh-leaf) has a spicy, lemony flavor with green leafy notes; dill seed is stronger and lacks the green aspect. It has carminative, cooling, and digestive qualities. Use dill weed for delicate meats, such as fish, seafood, and poultry; or to bring out the forage flavors in darker meats. Use dill seed as part of an herbal rub, stuffing, soups, or stews.

Fennel

Fennel (*Foeniculum vulgare*) has tall stems that have finely divided leaves and small yellow flowers, and it produces thin seeds. The bulb is eaten as a vegetable; leaves, stems, and seeds are used as herb or spice in cooking. Fennel has antispasmodic, carminative, detoxifying, and digestive qualities. Use leaves in salads, sauces, or stuffings to accompany wild game or free-range meats; they complement pork, veal, squirrel, rabbit, or fish. Sweeter stems go in salads or stir-fries. Pungent seeds go into sausages, pickles, and curries especially with lamb or duck.

French Tarragon

French tarragon (*Artemisia dracunculus*) is a bushy plant has slim gray-green leaves that are dried as a seasoning. It has antiseptic, digestive, and soothing qualities; and it freshens breath. French tarragon works well alone, though it also blends with lemony flavors. It goes well on veal, pork, rabbit, and venison. Use it in tartar sauce and other cream or mayonnaise sauces.

Garlic

Garlic (*Allium sativum*) has strappy leaves and a large edible bulb. The bulb divides into cloves which are usually chopped for their pungent, musky flavor. Cloves may also be roasted, or slivered and stuck into slits on a roast. Garlic has antibacterial, antiviral, carminative, detoxifying, digestive, and pest-repellent qualities. Use to flavor butter or sauces for seafood and fish. Stands up to robust meats such as lamb, goat, beef, or elk.

Ginger

Ginger (*Zingiber officinale*) has deep green leaves that rise above a thick rhizome. Ginger root is peeled and used fresh for its golden heat. Powdered ginger is milder, with a warm, dusty flavor. It has antiseptic, carminative, cleansing, stimulating, and warming qualities; it also serves as a "carrier" to spread other herbs through the body. Use fresh ginger for hot sauces and curries surrounding darker meats such as lamb, goat, beef, elk, or buffalo. It also makes an excellent glaze when combined with fruit, especially for pork or poultry. Powdered ginger works also with more delicate meats such as fish, seafood, squirrel, rabbit, or poultry. Pickled ginger slices pep up hot dogs or hamburgers. Ginger beer is a fine beverage to serve with small game.

Juniper

Juniper (*Juniperus communis*) is a prickly evergreen shrub or tree bears small dark berries that can be dried for culinary or medicinal uses. Juniper berries have a balsamic, resinous flavor. Juniper has carminative, stimulating, and stomachic qualities. The flavor brings out the dark, wild notes in robust meats, such as buffalo, elk, venison, duck, and pheasant. Juniper also lends its flavor to gin. Gin and tonic is a pleasant summer beverage with cold sliced meats.

Lemon Balm

Lemon balm (*Melissa officinalis*) is a member of the mint family. It bears oval leaves with scalloped edges and has a strong lemon flavor with green herbal notes. Use fresh or dried. It has antibacterial, antiviral, carminative, and digestive qualities. Excellent for its lemon flavor with fish, poultry, or rabbit. Brings out herbal notes in grass-fed beef or lamb. Also good in salads, with fruit, or as a garnish. It makes a nice tea.

Lemon Grass

Lemon grass (*Cymbopogon citratum*) is a yellow-green tropical grass with lemon and grassy flavors. Usually sold in dried form, but can be used fresh. Lemon grass has antinausea, cooling, digestive, and stimulating qualities. Use to flavor soups, salads, or curries; good for its lemon flavor with poultry or rabbit. Lay a bed of lemon grass under fish for grilling. Brings out herbal notes in grass-fed meats.

Mustard

Mustard (*Sinapis hirta*, *Brassica juncea*, *B. nigra*) is a small plant that bears bright yellow flowers, which produce many seeds with a sharp hot flavor. Mustard has antiseptic, carminative, digestive, stimulating, and warming qualities. Use a few whole seeds in soups, stews, etc. A pinch or two of powdered mustard adds zest to casseroles, meatloaf, or other blended dishes. Mustard paste makes a good sauce or glaze base for strong meats, such as beef and elk, or really exotic things like javelina that need to be spiced into submission.

Olive

Olive (*Olea europaea*) is a Mediterranean tree that bears small fruits that are picked green or black. Olives are preserved or pressed for their mellow or tangy oil. The oil has antioxidant, cleansing, and digestive qualities. Green olives are good as garnishes; black olives are excellent in stuffings or as toppings on a game pizza. Olives may also be stuffed with meat pastes. Olive oil is excellent for cooking seafood and lean meats, such as grass-fed beef, rabbit, or venison. Use "mild" oil for delicate meats or full-flavored "virgin" or "extra-virgin" oil for stronger meats.

Parsley

Parsley (*Petroselinum crispum*) is a dark green bushy herb that can have either flat or tightly crinkled leaves. Flavor is sharp and green with bitter notes. It has anti-inflamatory, antispasmodic, carminative, cleansing, digestive, and stimulating qualities. Excellent in salads and dressings, or chopped as a topping for soups or curries. Add to meatballs, burgers, and other blended recipes. Include in stuffings for fish or poultry.

Pepper

Pepper (*Piper nigrum*) is a tropical vine that produces tiny fruits, which are picked unripe and then dried. Black, white, green, and red peppercorns are available; each has its own flavor. Pepper may be purchased ground or whole. It has carminative, stimulating, and warming qualities. Black is the hottest, good for strong meats like beef, goat, and elk. White is hot, but mellower; use it on poultry, rabbit, pork, or fish. Green has a tangy, herbal heat ideal for poultry, fish, or grass-fed meats; it brings out leafy green notes in meat. Red is mild and fruity, nice with chicken, rabbit, pork, or venison.

Peppermint

Peppermint (*Mentha piperita*) is a leafy plant with slightly pointed oval leaves gives a strong blue minty flavor. It has antibacterial, antispasmodic, carminative, cooling, stimulating, and stomachic qualities; it also relieves bad breath. Peppermint makes an excellent cold tea for warm weather. Mint jelly is a traditional condiment for lamb. Mint also works well with delicate meats like poultry, fish, or rabbit.

Rose Hip

Rose hips (*Rosa spp.*) are the fruit produced on rose bushes. Rose hip has a tart fruity flavor. It has anti-inflamatory, astringent, and digestive qualities. Use rose hips for making sauces, syrups, or jellies; these are excellent condiments for use with wild meats or lamb. Also good in fruit-based meat recipes that use chicken or rabbit. Makes a delicious hot tea for accompanying dark meats.

Rosemary

Rosemary (*Rosmarinus officinalis*) is a woody herb that produces narrow needles that are dried for their piney, resinous flavor. It has antibiotic, astringent, digestive, relaxing, restorative, and tonic qualities. Use dried leaves to bring out the complexities in robust meats such as beef, buffalo, or venison. Twigs stripped of leaves may be used as shish kebob skewers for added flavor.

Sage

Sage (*Salvia officinalis*) is a small woody bush with leathery gray-green leaves. Its flavor is musky, herbal, resinous, and camphoraceous. It has antidepressant, antiseptic, astringent, carminative, digestive, relaxing, and tonic qualities. Use its dried leaves in soups, stews, sauces, etc. It goes well with dark meats such as turkey, duck, beef, lamb, or venison.

Thyme

Thyme (*Thymus vulgaris, T. citriodorus, T. herba-barona*) is a tiny bush that bears minute green leaves that have a musky herbal flavor. Some varieties have other flavors such as lemon thyme or caraway thyme. It has antiseptic, astringent, carminative, digestive, and relaxing qualities. Use the leaves in soups, marinades, gravies, stuffings, or casseroles. Thyme complements most meats, including poultry, pork, rabbit, and squirrel. Lemon thyme is especially good for fish. Caraway thyme is ideal for dark meats such as beef, goat, or elk.

Wild and Free-Range Recipes

Herbs and spices combine in many different ways. They can be sprinkled onto whole meat, tucked under wrappings, blended into meat mixtures, and so forth. The following recipes are versatile, to give you an idea of what you can do. Shift the seasonings a bit and you can adapt these basic recipes to more types of meat.

Campfire Fish Rub

Combine equal amounts of dried dill weed, lemon balm, and thyme (preferably lemon thyme) in a shaker bottle. Add salt and ground pepper to taste; roughly a teaspoon of each into an average-sized herb bottle is about right. All this fits in one bottle for easy packing, and it enhances most types of fish. Sprinkle onto freshly cleaned whole fish or fillets before cooking; it works whether you are cooking fish over open flames or wrapping it in aluminum foil to bake in the coals.

Forest Roast

3–4 pound roast of venison, elk, etc.

½ teaspoon dried rosemary

½ teaspoon dried sage

½ teaspoon green peppercorns

½ teaspoon cayenne

8 juniper berries

½ pound fatty bacon

1. Preheat oven to 325°F. Grease a baking dish that is slightly larger than the roast.

2. Rinse roast, pat dry, and place on cutting board.

3. In a small bowl, grind together dried rosemary, dried sage, green peppercorns, cayenne, and juniper berries. Sprinkle over roast, coating all sides thoroughly.

4. Separate the strips of fatty bacon. Wrap spiced roast completely in bacon strips, then place roast in baking dish.

5. Cover dish loosely with aluminum foil.

6. Cook for about 2½ hours.

Serves 6 to 8.

Grass-Fed Beef Loaf

For Loaf:

1 pound grass-fed ground beef or veal

1 free-range egg

2 handfuls organic saltine crackers, crushed

2 garlic cloves, minced

1 tablespoon fresh minced parsley

1 teaspoon fresh minced sage

½ teaspoon dried lemon grass

½ teaspoon sea salt (or plain table salt)

For Topping:

½ teaspoon dried rosemary

¼ teaspoon black peppercorns

A pinch of caraway seeds

¼ cup organic ketchup

1. Preheat oven to 350°F. Grease a loaf pan.

2. In a large bowl, knead together all ingredients for the loaf. Shape the meat mixture into an oval and place it in the loaf pan.

3. In a small bowl, crush together dried rosemary, black peppercorns, and a pinch of caraway seeds. Add organic ketchup. Brush half of the topping over the loaf.

4. Cook loaf for 55 minutes. Remove loaf from oven; brush remaining sauce over the top. Return loaf to oven for 5 minutes.

Serves 4 to 5.

Poultry with Wild Rice

Olive oil

4 skinless, boneless breast pieces (duck, turkey, grouse, etc.), 6 to 8 ounces each

Powdered ginger

Salt

1 onion, chopped

3 celery ribs, chopped

3 cups broth (chicken, turkey, etc.)

6 ounces shiitake or other mushrooms

6 ounces long grain and wild rice

¼ cup fresh parsley, chopped

½ teaspoon green peppercorns

½ teaspoon dried sage

Pinch of fennel seeds

1. Preheat oven to 350°F. Grease a casserole dish with olive oil and set aside. Pour a little more olive oil into a skillet and start it heating.

2. Rinse and pat dry poultry breasts. Sprinkle with powdered ginger and salt. Lay them in the skillet with chopped onion and chopped celery. Sauté until breasts are browned on all sides and vegetables begin to soften. With a slotted spatula, transfer the breasts and vegetables into the casserole dish.

3. In a bowl, combine broth, mushrooms, long-grain and wild rice, fresh parsley, green peppercorns, dried sage, and fennel seeds. Pour over the breasts and vegetables.

4. Cover casserole dish and cook at 350°F for 1½ to 2 hours, until rice has absorbed broth and breasts are done.

Serves 4.

Quick Cuisine

❧ by Dallas Jennifer Cobb ❧

D o you rush to get everything done after work and before dinner, only to realize you don't have anything easy to prepare on hand? Want to learn a few recipes for quick herb wonders that will save you time, energy, money, and make you feel like a gourmet cook?

A quick meal that is good for you is a life saver, and the fewer dishes to do after, the better. These recipes for quick herb cuisine are just that—good, quick, and easy. And all of them contain tasty, nutritious herbs. Because they take little time for preparation, you can whip them up before your blood sugar plummets or your hungry family decides to order out. Because they involve very few dishes,

you can relax at the table and savor the food, knowing that cleanup will also be quick and easy.

Inspired by my busy life, I have developed a number of recipes that I rely on to produce healthy meals that are fast, tasty, and easy to prepare. My "quick" repertoire includes a little bit of everything, so I have included tried and true recipes for salad dressings, breads and biscuits, treats, and savory, fast meals.

These recipes will not only make your life a little easier, they will give you a reputation as a gourmet cook of great (quick) cuisine.

Quick Cuisine Basics

"Quick" doesn't have to mean TV dinners or microwaved processed food. Quick can become synonymous with good when you learn a few tricks. Preparing good quality quick cuisine is easy with good tools and a few staple gourmet items in your fridge.

I love to cook in one or two pots, so there is less to wash up. Less is better. With just two versatile tools, you can make a wide variety of quick, nutritious, gourmet meals. I think that everyone should own a stainless steel steamer set and a good quality no-stick frying pan. A steamer can be used for most meals, making the preparation of vegetables quick and nutritious. After bringing a cup of water to boil in the bottom, add all your favorite chopped vegetables on top, and steam for less than 2 minutes. Don't overcook! Use three different colored vegetables for maximum visual impact and nutrition.

A no-stick frying pan can be used to prepare many of the main course savory recipes below. It is easy to clean and highly versatile. A heavier weight pan will hold its heat, cooking with better results.

The staple gourmet items kept in my fridge include a variety of herb butters for quick additions to fish, biscuits, and pastas, a simple salad dressing with complex tastes, and pesto sauce made from fresh basil and garlic. Let's start with the recipes for these three quick cuisine staples.

Gourmet Herb Butters

½ pound of butter, room temperature

Fresh herbs, finely minced

Blend butter and fresh herbs together in the food processor, then spatula out into a re-sealable container for storage in the fridge.

Gourmet garlic butter calls for 2 cloves of finely minced garlic and a tablespoon of chopped chives.

Provençal butter calls for ½ teaspoon each of fresh basil, thyme, sage, oregano, and lavender (herbs that commonly grow in the Provence region of France). Provençal herb mixes are also widely available in grocery stores. Rub Provençal butter on chicken prior to roasting for crisp delicious tasting skin.

Cilantro herb butter calls for ½ teaspoon of finely grated lemon peel, a tablespoon of finely chopped cilantro, and one clove of garlic finely minced.

Herbed butters are easy to make and delicious. You can whip up something gourmet in just a few minutes, and keep it in the fridge in a sealed container for weeks. Make a few varieties to keep on hand for easy versatility. If you are vegan, you can use margarine instead with good results.

Easy Herb Balsamic Dressing

½ cup balsamic vinegar

⅛ cup olive oil

⅛ cup maple syrup—you can use honey if maple syrup isn't available in your area

¼ cup water

1 teaspoon mustard powder (use prepared mustard if you must)

Mix everything in a big jar and shake well. Store the jar in the fridge. For instant gourmet dressing, remove from fridge before the meal and shake before use.

A gorgeous gourmet salad can be made by dressing romaine leaves with balsamic dressing and sprinkling with calendula petals or any other brightly colored edible flower.

Presto Pesto

3 cups fresh basil leaves

1½ cups chopped walnuts

4 cloves garlic, peeled

¼ cup grated Romano goat cheese

½ cup + olive oil (I like a thick sauce, you may prefer more oil)

Salt and pepper to taste

In a food processor, blend basil, nuts, garlic, and cheese. Add oil slowly while mixing. Add salt and pepper.

Pesto can be kept in the fridge for a week and almost indefinitely in the freezer. You can freeze cubes in an ice cube tray for quick use in recipes. One of my favorite healthy recipes is Pesto Pasta.

Pesto Pasta

Dry pasta noodles (enough for 4 people)

1 cup of Presto Pesto

1½ cups each chopped broccoli, cauliflower, and green beans, chopped (or use your favorite vegetables for variety)

Grated Romano goat cheese to taste

1. Boil water in the bottom of your steamer, add pasta.

3. While pasta cooks, quickly steam veggies over top.

4. Place cooked pasta and veggies in a large mixing bowl and add a cup of Presto Pesto. Mix, and serve with goat Romano sprinkled on top.

Makes enough pasta for four people. If you want added protein, both chicken and shrimp go well with this recipe.

Heavenly Herb Biscuits

2 cups flour

4½ teaspoons baking powder

½ teaspoon salt

3 tablespoons butter (or margarine for a vegan version)

1 cup milk (or use almond or soymilk for the vegan version)

1. Mix dry ingredients together in a large bowl.

2. Carefully cut in butter (or margarine), using your fingertips to add it to the dry ingredients.

3. Form a hole in the center of the dry ingredients, pour the milk in and slowly mix to form a soft dough. Give

it a few quick kneads on a floured board, then pat down to about half an inch thick, and cut with a floured knife or cutter.

4. Place on an oiled cookie sheet, and bake at 450°F for 12 to 15 minutes.

Serve warm with gourmet garlic butter or a favorite topping.

Use different kinds of flour in this recipe to produce different textures and flavors. My favorite mix is half spelt and half whole wheat, but my family loves it when I use all oat flour, which makes for a very traditional Scottish biscuit taste.

Herbs add variety to these biscuits and create complementary tastes for different dishes. To accompany pork or poultry, add 1½ teaspoons fresh minced sage (or ¼ teaspoon dried) and 1½ teaspoons fresh thyme (or ¼ teaspoon dried). To accompany Italian food, make a zesty garlic biscuit by mixing in 4 cloves of finely minced fresh garlic and a tablespoon of finely minced fresh parsley.

For scones, leave out the salt and milk, substituting ¼ cup of sugar, and ¾ cup of cream for a sweet biscuit that's ideal with jam, honey or orange butter.

Quick Herb Cuisine at Home

With two quick tools, a few herb basics in the fridge, and these recipes, you are off to a good start. The next time you feel like you need to eat right now, don't reach for fast food, chocolate, or cookies. Take a minute to whip up some quick herb cuisine and reward yourself with good tasting, nutritious food that is fast and easy.

Delectable, Edible Herb Flowers

❧ by Suzanne Ress ❧

Most herb plants have strongly aromatic leaves that are useful in cooking. All herb plants produce flowers, and flowers produce seeds—dill, caraway, coriander, anise, fennel, nigella, cumin, and others—that we value as culinary seasonings. Did you know that artichokes, capers, and asparagus are also flowers? Some herbs—basil, rosemary, horehound, sage, thyme, bergamot, mint, costmary, wormwood, southernwood, and tarragon, for example—also have flowers that lend themselves particularly well to recipes for food and drinks.

Preparing foods and drinks with flowers can take your love of herb gardening to a new level. Beyond appreciating herbal flowers for their visual beauty and alluring scents, you can relish their flavors and nutritional attributes as well.

Not all herb flowers are edible, though. Purple loosestrife, black hellebore, and lily of the valley are extremely poisonous. Sometimes, cultivars of an edible herbal flower become inedible, and even mildly poisonous, through overcultivation. Always be certain to correctly identify your herbal plants by their Latin names, as common names can vary according to where you live and/or obtain your plants. One example of name confusion is the herbal flower known as "pot marigold." Its Latin name is *Calendula officinalis*, and it is also commonly known as calendula. This plant's flowers are useful and very edible. Unfortunately, calendula can be confused with the plant usually called "marigold" (*Tagetes*), a pretty garden flower that is not edible at all!

Be sure of what you are eating, and also know your source. If you grow herbs and herbal flowers yourself, you can be certain that no pesticides, fungicides, or other chemical treatments that can make flowers unsafe for human consumption have been used. Do not be tempted to gather flowers from public gardens to use in food and drink, for you never know what poisons they may have been treated with.

Before picking herbal flowers, spray them gently with water to remove soil and tiny insects.

Herbal flowers can be used in everything from beverages to appetizers and pastas, rice dishes, crepes, soups, soufflés, quiches and omelets; with fish, meat, and poultry; in salads, sauces, desserts, jams and jellies; in pickles, after-dinner drinks, and even candied. Here are a few of the many edible flowers that are available to you.

Borage

Borage (*Borago officinalis*) is an annual herb plant that produces bright blue star-shaped flowers all summer long that have a fresh taste similar to cucumber. You can sprinkle a handful of borage blossoms over a green salad for a magical appearance, or float a few in a glass of white wine for the same effect. Or they can be used to make this refreshing summer appetizer:

Celery Stuffed with Borage Blossoms

A big bunch of fresh, crisp celery

6 ounces softened brie

3 ounces softened butter

A large handful of borage blossoms, plus a few more to decorate

Black peppercorns for grinding, optional

1. Separate, wash, and trim the celery stalks, and cut them into 4-inch pieces.

2. Carefully trim away the white crust from the brie, and put the rest into a food processor together with the butter. Blend until soft and spreadable.

3. Roughly chop the handful of borage blossoms (saving some to decorate), and gently mix them into the cheese, using a wooden spoon. Fill each celery stalk piece with this blue and white cream.

4. Place all the stalks upon a dish of romaine lettuce, scatter a few more borage blossoms over all, grind on some black pepper, and serve.

Calendula

Calendula (*Calendula officinalis*) has pretty, deep golden-yellow flowers. The petals and buds of calendula can be scattered over salads, deviled eggs, risottos, or pasta dishes to add color. Or you might try baking this festive dessert.

Calendula Chess Pie

Ingredients for pie crust:

1½ cups flour

¾ teaspoon salt

½ cup cold unsalted butter

Ice water

Preheat oven to 350°F.

1. Sift the flour and salt into a bowl.

2. Use a pastry cutter or two knives to cut the cold butter into the mixture until it resembles coarse sand.

3. Add ice-cold water, one tablespoon at a time, and blending each time with a fork until the mixture holds together as a ball.

4. Chill the dough in the refrigerator while you prepare the filling.

Ingredients for filling:

1 cup butter

1 cup light honey

4 eggs

1 teaspoon grated lemon rind

1 tablespoon calendula flower petals

1 tablespoon finely chopped red shiso leaf

½ teaspoon cinnamon

1. Cream the butter and honey together until smooth.

2. Add the eggs, and beat well until frothy.

3. Stir in the grated lemon rind, calendula petals, cinnamon, and chopped shiso leaf.

4. Remove the chilled dough from the fridge and roll it out on a floured surface. Transfer it to your pie pan and flute the edges.

5. Pour the pie filling into the crust and bake for 40 minutes.

Serve warm or cold.

Chamomile

The calming effect of chamomile (*Chamaemelum nobile* or *Matricaria recutita*) flower tea is well-known, but have you ever thought of making a chamomile liquor?

Soothing Chamomile Liquor

To make a liquor, put ⅔ cup of whole fresh or dried chamomile flowers, stems removed, into a quart-sized mason jar. Pour 3 cups of 95-proof alcohol over the chamomile flowers. Add a 2-inch piece of orange or tangerine peel with white part removed. Leave this to macerate for one month, shaking it gently once a week or so.

After a month, prepare syrup, as follows:
1. Mix together 3 cups water, 1½ cups sugar, and 1 cup clear light honey. Stir over medium heat until the sugar

is completely dissolved and the mixture begins to simmer. Leave the syrup to cool completely.

2. While the syrup is cooling, strain the chamomile flowers, orange (or tangerine) rind out of the alcohol. Add the strained liquid to the syrup and mix.

3. Use a funnel and pour the liquor into clean attractive bottles. Close the bottles and keep them undisturbed in a cool, dry place for at least a month before trying this excellent nightcap.

Fennel

Fennel (*Foeniculum vulgare*), also called wild fennel, does not produce a fennel bulb like the cultivated vegetable fennel plants do. It does produce many beautiful umbels of tiny yellow flowers, however, which later turn into fennel seeds. The pollen of wild fennel flowers is considered a great delicacy when sprinkled over fish. The fresh or dried flowers can also be used to make vinegar to use in Potato Salad with Fennel and Chive Flowers.

Note: The fennel flower vinegar is made in advance, so plan ahead for the following recipe.

Potato Salad with Fennel and Chive Flowers

1 pound red skinned potatoes, washed, peeled, and cut into ½-inch cubes

⅓ cup olive oil

1 teaspoon grated lemon rind

2 tablespoons fennel flower vinegar

Salt and pepper

Small bunch of chives, finely chopped, plus several chive blossoms

6 ounces feta cheese

1. Bring a large pot of salted water to a boil and toss in the diced potatoes. Keep the water boiling and cook for only 8 minutes, then immediately drain.

2. While potatoes are cooking, stir together in a small bowl the olive oil, grated lemon rind, vinegar, salt, and pepper.

3. Put the warm potatoes into a serving bowl and mix them gently but thoroughly with the olive oil mixture.

4. After the potato mixture is cool, stir in the fennel flowers, chopped chives, and crumbled feta. Mix well. Decorate with a few chive blossoms.

5. Chill well before serving.

Fennel Flower Vinegar
(Make in advance.)

5 or 6 fennel umbels

White wine vinegar

1. Carefully remove the flowers from the fennel umbels and place umbels in a half-quart size canning jar.

2. Cover with good quality white wine vinegar, close the jar, and leave to macerate for two weeks.

3. After two weeks, filter the vinegar (using cheesecloth over a funnel) into an attractive bottle or vinegar carafe.

Lavender

Lavender (*Lavandula augustifolia*) is one of my favorite perennial herb flowers. It has a long blooming time, lacy-looking blue flowers, and a clean, fresh scent. The intriguing aroma of lavender is similar in some ways to rosemary, but more feminine. Lavender pairs well with chicken.

Chicken with Lavender Flowers

½ bottle dry white wine

3 tablespoon lavender flowers, stems removed

2 cloves garlic, chopped fine

Pepper

1 whole chicken, cut into serving size pieces

1 teaspoon thyme

1 tablespoon olive oil

1 tablespoon butter

½ cup chicken broth

½ cup black olives

1. Mix together wine, lavender flowers, garlic, thyme and pepper to make marinade. Place chicken pieces in a sealable container. Pour marinade over chicken. Cover and refrigerate overnight, or about 8 hours.

2. Next day, heat the olive oil and butter together in a large, heavy-bottomed pan over medium heat. When the butter has melted, remove the chicken pieces from the marinade (reserve marinade) and place in a pan with the olive oil-butter mixture. Cook chicken pieces on all sides until golden.

3. Add together the reserved marinade, remaining spices, and the chicken broth. Pour over chicken and bring to a simmer.

4. Cover the pan and leave the chicken to simmer until cooked through, about 20 minutes.

5. Scatter the black olives over all, remove from heat.

6. Serve with plenty of fresh, crusty bread.

Nasturtium

I love nasturtium (*Tropaeolum majus*) flowers and leaves in salad. They are so bright, unexpected, and deliciously fresh-tasting. You can use just about any salad greens, but the best are ones you've grown yourself. Try using a sweet butterhead lettuce, or a fresh romaine, or a red-tinged lolla rossa, plus watercress, arugula, fresh basil leaves, and other fresh chopped herbs from your garden. Rinse and drain all the greens well, tear into bite-sized pieces, and toss in 8 to 10 red, yellow, and orange nasturtium flowers for a really exciting salad. You can also add a few blue borage blossoms, yellow pansies, wild purple violets, and red or pink rose petals to the salad if you want to make it extra fancy and magical. Dress with a simple vinaigrette made from olive oil, lemon juice, salt, and pepper just before serving.

Sweet Woodruff

You can use either fresh or dried sweet woodruff (*Gallium odoratum*) flowers and leaves, but the dried ones have more flavor. Try this very old traditional festive German drink served at Walpurgis Night and May Day.

May Wine Punch

1 bottle sweet white German wine

3 ounces fresh or 1 ounce dried sweet woodruff leaves and flowers

½ cup sugar

1 cup brandy

½ cup wild strawberries

1 orange, deseeded and thinly sliced

1 bottle dry champagne

2 or 3 sprigs of fresh sweet woodruff flowers for garnish

1. Pour the white wine into a glass bowl and add the sweet woodruff. Cover and leave it to macerate for 24 hours.

2. Prepare syrup by mixing ½ cup sugar with 1 cup water. Gradually heat until sugar dissolves and syrup simmers. Cool.

3. Strain the macerated wine and discard the sweet woodruff.

4. Put the strained wine, cooled syrup, brandy, sliced orange, and wild strawberries into a chilled punch bowl, and keep cool.

5. Just before serving, add the bottle of champagne, and float little white, starry, sweet woodruff flowers on top.

Royal Basil

❧ by Harmony Usher ❧

B asil has quite a royal reputation to live up to. The revered
"king of herbs" is known
botanically as *Ocimum Basilicum*, a
name derived from *basileus*, which
is the Greek word for king. Other
translations of its name include "fit
for a king" or "magnificent."

In Greek folklore, it was said that
only the king was permitted to grow
and harvest basil, and harvesting
was to be done only with a golden
sickle. In addition to its esteemed
culinary qualities, basil has been revered for its essential oil and used
to create perfumes reserved only for
royal families. It was also used by the
Greek Orthodox Church to create

Basil

holy water, and ancient Egyptians used basil in the embalming of mummies.

Basil's name also alludes to a Roman legend connecting it to the cure for the bite of a basilisk—a terrifying mythological creature with the head of a rooster, body of a serpent, and wings of a bat. Basil was said to be the only cure for the basilisk's bite and breath, which were believed to have the power to kill both plants and animals.

Other royal associations include the reported relationship between basil and Tulasi, wife of the Hindu god Vishnu. The legend says that when Tulasi came to earth, she did so in the form of basil. Because of this, many Hindus see the herb as sacred and ask forgiveness when they touch it.

Known as "tulsi" in Ayurvedic medicine, "Holy" basil has been used in India for thousands of years to treat fever, inflammation, malaria, dysentery, diarrhea, constipation, indigestion, bronchitis, bronchial asthma, arthritis, insect bites, skin conditions, and eye diseases. To this day its essential oils are sought after for a variety of healing applications and natural health remedies.

Basil's Royal Qualities

Basil is a tender, low-growing perennial in the mint family. It has been growing wild for thousands of years in India, Iran, Africa, and Asia. Basil's reign as a cultivated herb appears to have begun about three thousand years ago in these same places, arriving in England and other parts of Europe closer to the Middle Ages. The sheer number of varieties is notable, with between forty and sixty types found around the world.

In North American, we are most familiar with sweet basil—a bright green, large-leafed variety that lends its bold spicy-sweet flavor to cooking. Other varieties include "Purple Ruffles," "Lemon basil", and "Lettuce Leaf basil".

Sweet basil can be found in its fresh form in most urban grocery stores. The dried kind, which is popularly used in combination with oregano and parsley in Italian cooking, can be found just about anywhere. Other varieties, such as "Globe basil" and "Thai basil", have been gaining popularity as our exposure to global cooking styles and our desire to try new foods have grown. These can be found in urban markets and specialty Eastern-food shops.

I think most would agree that its basil's bold flavor and divine scent that make it so "kingly." You need only brush against basil in the garden on a hot July afternoon to be subject to its rule. Although the scents and flavors differ across varieties, many have notes of anise, pepper, lemon, or cinnamon.

Basil becomes majestic when added to a freshly harvested green salad, and can be laid across soft cheeses, such as brie or camembert, in a baguette for a picnic lunch that will refuse to be forgotten. Basil is a lover of fresh tomatoes, and it has long been used in Italian cooking as a desired companion to "Beefsteaks" and "Best Boys".

As there are so many varieties—some boasting nuances of chocolate or lemon—there are infinite possibilities in food combining and experimentation. The health conscious should note that basil also contains respectable amounts of beta carotene, calcium, and vitamin C, particularly when eaten fresh and whole.

Princely Pesto

Pesto is a blended mixture of nuts, cheese, oil, and herbs. It is usually made, easily and quickly, in a home blender. It is the perfect way to capture the fresh flavor of basil and keep it long after its limited growing season is over. Basil pesto is most common, where the herb is traditionally combined with fresh Parmesan cheese, pine nuts, olive oil, and garlic to create a rich spread that can be used in a variety of ways. The ratio of each ingredient can be altered to taste and taking into consideration its final use. If you are concerned about calories, vegetable stock can be used to replace some of the oil; cheese can be low fat, reduced, or eliminated altogether; and fewer nuts can be used.

In my humble opinion, pesto is the easiest and most effective way to raise even the most customary meal to regal heights. This is because pesto can be made when basil is freshly harvested and kept for a long time in a closed container in the fridge, or for an indefinite amount of time in the freezer when it is tightly sealed. When thawed, the flavor remains almost as fresh as the day the basil was harvested!

Pesto is delightful and rich when spread on simple fresh bread (such as a baguette) and topped with tomatoes, grilled vegetables, or soft cheeses. With the cost of both pine nuts and cheese in a traditional pesto, it is good to know that a small dollop, thinly spread, goes a long way! You can also do some substitutions to reduce cost, such as replacing the high-priced pine nuts with the more modestly priced walnut, or by using processed Parmesan instead of the fresh variety from the deli.

Pesto can also be used in pasta dishes—stirred into the noodles just before serving and topped with a little extra cheese. One of our favorite ways to enjoy pesto in our household is to stir it into brown rice just before the rice is served. The combination of the pesto with the nuttiness of the brown rice is a divine combination that will have family and guests requesting more.

Basil pesto can be used to top steamed vegetables, fish, or chicken. It can also be used in a variety of vegetarian bean, lentil, or grain dishes.

A Standard Pesto Recipe

2 cups fresh basil leaves

2 cloves fresh garlic, minced

½ cup grated Romano or Parmesan cheese

½ cup olive oil

¼ cup pine nuts

Place ingredients in blender, adding half the oil to begin, and adding the rest slowly as you use the "pulse" feature to avoid over-blending. Experiment with amounts of each ingredient and with substitutions, as desired.

Basil Brown Rice with Black Beans

1 cup brown rice

2 tablespoons prepared pesto

1 cup fresh basil, chopped

1 cup black beans, warmed

1. Prepare 1 cup of brown rice per directions. In the final ten minutes of cooking, stir in 2 tablespoons of prepared pesto.

2. Add 1 cup of chopped, fresh basil to the pot and allow it to steam on top of the rice (with the lid still on).

3. When the rice is finished cooking, lightly toss the now-steamed basil into the rice.

4. Add 1 cup of warm black beans to the dish and serve.

A side of steamed zucchini and peppers makes this a complete and very satisfying meal.

Basil Oil

> 2 cups of basil leaves, fresh from the garden, rinsed, and patted dry
>
> 1 cup of high quality olive oil, room temperature

1. Combine basil and olive oil in blender.

2. Blend until leaves are just finely chopped. You still want to be able to see the leaves.

3. Pour in a sauce pan and heat until the oil begins to boil, and then simmer for about 5 minutes.

4. Remove from heat and let stand until cooled.

5. Strain the oil through cheesecloth and discard basil.

6. Store in an airtight container for up to three months.

It will be a challenge to return to plain oil after sampling this delightful rendition! Enjoy as a base for salad dressing, drizzled over fresh tomatoes and goat cheese, or as a topping for a divine bruschetta.

Growing Basil

The best way to guarantee a fresh supply of this stately herb is to grow it at home. Like a discriminating monarch, however, it requires your focused attention to environment and care, and it will tolerate nothing less. This is not an herb that mingles with commoners!

Basil succumbs at even the mention of frost and is best kept under glass (inside the castle) until all such threats have passed. It is not easy to grow from seed, but with patience and attention (and care not to under- or over-water) it can be coaxed along until it can be put out of doors.

Basil likes rich, loamy soil in a warm, still location. It companions well with tomatoes. I have had good success with basil when I planted it along a south-facing brick wall, where the heat retained by the bricks during the day keeps the basil warm through the night. Be careful to keep the area clear of weeds, however, as earwigs have a hunger for basil and will hide in the garden refuse at the base of the plants, emerging and eating the leaves under the cover of night.

If you successfully create an environment that allows for basil's growth, do take time to "pinch off" the plant regularly to encourage new, thicker growth and make sure to remove any flowers that begin forming. Once the plant has flowered, all of its energy goes into producing seed, leaving you with fewer leaves to cook with. I harvest from the top of the plant as I need it, which seems to encourage a thickening of the greens. Basil's leaves bruise easily after harvesting, so treat them gently, and unless you plan to dry them, use soon after harvesting.

Storing Basil

Because basil loses a great deal of its flavor when dried, freezing is a better alternative. To freeze, take stems of fresh basil and dip into boiling water for only a few seconds. Dip right away in a bowl of ice water, take the leaves from the stem, pat dry, and flash freeze them on a cookie sheet. Once it's frozen, store the basil in an airtight container.

One More Kingly Recipe

You can also add blanched basil to butter. Stir it into the butter or blend with an electric blender. Then, using wax paper, roll the butter-basil mix into logs that can be frozen and then cut into "pats" of butter as needed.

Another alternative is to use the blender once again. Blend basil with a bit of water, pour into ice cube trays and freeze. These can be popped out of the trays and put into airtight containers in the freezer and used through the winter for soups, stews, rice, and pasta dishes.

If you are looking for ways to elevate your daily cooking from pedestrian to imperial, basil is clearly your herb. Here is to wishing you a successful growing season, and a year of dining with the king of herbs!

Herbs
for
Health
and
Beauty

Energy-Opening Herbs

≫ Tess Whitehurst ≪

Modern science now agrees with what traditional healers have always known: we dwell in a sea of energy. We are surrounded by energy and comprised of energy. It naturally follows that all healing modalities are concerned with positively affecting the quality of our energy. In other words, when our energy flows through our minds, bodies, and environments in an ideal way, we are nourished on every level.

We are all, whether we realize it or not, conscious of the quality of our personal energy and the energy of that which surrounds us. This can be proved by the number of popular linguistic expressions that describe these qualities (which we all intuitively understand right away) such as "wired," "amped up," "drained," "burned out," "going with the flow," "grounded," "wishy-washy," "stale," "bubbly," "swimming upstream," "fizzled," and "full of life."

Of course, sometimes, energy doesn't flow in an ideal way because it gets "stuck." For example, our emotional energy might get stuck, in which case we might feel depressed. Or the energy of our internal organs might get stuck, in which case we might have trouble digesting or eliminating properly. It could also happen that our sexual energy gets stuck, which might cause us to feel disconnected from our physical desires and sensuality.

Interestingly, for any way that our energy might get stuck, there is an herb that can help "unstick" it.

Energy Openers

The following herbs are famous "energy openers," known for their unique abilities to dissolve and dissipate stagnant conditions in order to get energy flowing in a healthy way.

Castor

Although it's not exactly pleasing to the taste buds, when taken internally, castor oil, which comes from the castor oil plant (*Ricinus communis*, a member of the spurge community), can clear stagnant energy and toxins from our bodies through its laxative and purgative action.

Edgar Cayce, the renowned psychic and healer, applied castor oil to his patients externally and praised it for its miraculous ability to cure a huge number of ailments by lifting and dispersing the stagnant energy at the root of the imbalance.

In India, some new mothers employ castor oil's energy opening action to get their breast milk flowing by applying it to their breasts soon after childbirth.

Cayenne

Cayenne is a quick and fiery jump-starter. Medicinally, it helps get digestive juices flowing, stimulates circulation, and offers a quick, overall energy boost. Practitioners of folk magic have been known to employ cayenne to disperse negativity and to invigorate their love lives with passion and heat.

Cedar

Simply gazing at a living cedar tree and inhaling its fresh scent can create feelings of strength, serenity, and calm. Cedar gives us a transfusion of life force energy ("prana" or "chi"); it enhances our personal power as well as the healing power of our bodies. Therefore, it should come as no surprise that the name cedar comes from the Arabic word *kedron*, which means "power."

When mixed with a carrier oil and massaged into the body, essential oil of cedar can help loosen chest congestion and lend strength to the kidneys and spleen. When diffused or inhaled, cedar oil clears the mind, strengthens the resolve, and increases inspiration and motivation, which help to elevate us out of emotional ruts.

Damiana

Damiana is an herbal energy opener gets energy moving on all fronts. In addition to boosting mood by propelling us out of depressive ruts, soothing and healing our urinary flow, and acting as a mild laxative, it's perhaps one of the best-known herbal aphrodisiacs. Damiana enflames passion, enhances sensuality, and helps get us out of our heads and into our bodies.

In general, if you find yourself describing your mind, body, sex life, or all of the above as "stuck," damiana might be just the thing to help "unstick" you.

Desert Sage

Many of us are familiar with the Native American practice of burning sage bundles (smudging) to lift the vibes and clear personal energy fields or the energy field of an object or space. Desert sage, while similarly aromatic, is in a different family (*Artemisia*) than white and silver sages (*Salvia*) that are most commonly employed for this purpose. When burned as a smudge stick, desert sage clears the energy in a space just as powerfully, but in its own unique way.

When the energy of a person, place, or object is stale or stagnant, the smoke from desert sage can shift it immediately and powerfully. According to Native American tradition, it begins by infusing us with feelings of safety, familiarity, and hominess. Then it moves the energy around in a swirling, playful way, opening doors to new possibilities, ideas, and outlooks. It's perfect for clearing the space in your home after prolonged feelings of heaviness, despair, grief, discord, fear, and/or general "stuckness" in any or all life areas.

Eucalyptus

In addition to relieving congestion, opening up the breathing passages, and helping heal infections, the eucalyptus tree can even break up negative energetic conditions in its habitat. Its extreme need for water helps dry up swampy areas and reduce the spread of malaria. In aromatherapy, eucalyptus is employed to open up our perspective, invigorate the spirit, and dislodge limiting conditions, such as depression, anxiety, and low self-esteem.

Garlic

Garlic gets the energy moving in our bodies in several ways. It helps clear infections, fungus, and parasites; it gets the circulation flowing, and increases sweating to help purify the body of toxins; it aids the digestion and helps break up chest congestion and mucus.

In folk magic, garlic holds a special distinction as one of the most protective of all herbs. One of the ways it is said to protect is by dispersing negative energy and entities from an area.

Lemon

Lemons are famous for their freshness and potency, and their energy-opening power comes from their ability to powerfully clean and refresh our bodies (when consumed), our spirits and emotions (when inhaled), and our environments (when used as a cleaner or aromatic mist).

Medicinally, lemon is a general health tonic. It strengthens circulation, enhances the immune system, stimulates the liver, aids digestion, and supports overall detoxification.

Traditionally, lemon juice has been used to purify objects. It can be added to bath water to purify the spirit and offer an energetic boost. Employing lemon in any capacity is great for helping us heal from any situation, such as abuse that has caused us to feel used or contaminated.

Peppermint

When we're experiencing stagnant energy in our intestines (gas, bloating, and/or constipation) or chest (bronchial infections and/or phlegm) peppermint's unique ability to "unstick" might be just what the holistic health practitioner ordered.

Additionally, peppermint is a powerful internal cleanser. It's antibacterial and antifungal, and helps stimulate detoxification through sweating.

Mint has been touted as a spiritual energy opener for centuries by aromatherapy practitioners. Pliny stated that "the very smell of it alone recovers and refreshes the spirit. Similarly (but in more modern times), author Scott Cunningham suggested that peppermint is great for purifying the energy and lifting the vibrations of people, objects, and environments.

Senna

Among the strongest and most widely used herbal laxatives, senna is well known for moving stagnant matter swiftly and effectively out of the intestines.

Thyme

While thyme may not heal all wounds, it's definitely a very useful medicine. It has an opening, soothing, purifying action. It opens the bronchial passages (loosens congestion), soothes the muscles (reduces spasms), purifies the skin (helps heal fungal infections), and purifies the digestive tract (cleanses it of harmful bacteria and worms).

On the emotional and energetic levels, thyme is said to prevent nightmares, bolster courage, and purify a space of negative vibrations. Its pungent, magical, otherworldly scent can be employed to stimulate our creativity and help us to see any situation from a new and more helpful perspective.

Vervain

In both Eastern and Western herbal traditions, vervain is credited with abundant medicinal benefits. It's been used to relieve stress and nervous tension, aid digestion, strengthen the reproductive organs, and encourage the production of breast milk.

Additionally, in many cultures, a number of energy-opening magical properties have been ascribed to vervain.

In ancient Rome, bundles of vervain were used like brooms to sweep and energetically purify altars created for the god Jupiter. In the Middle Ages, vervain was carried to get one's luck flowing.

Vetiver

While most famed herbal energy openers seem to lean toward the pungently "yang" (masculine), vetiver's energy-opening action is gentler, softer, and more "yin" (feminine). In aromatherapy and folk magic, it has been employed to help us open up to abundance, beauty, and self-love by soothing our fears and insecurities, relaxing our bodies, reconnecting us to our senses, and reminding of the ever-present nourishment that Mother Earth provides.

Resources

Chevallier, Andrew. *Encyclopedia of Herbal Medicine*. New York: Dorling Kindersley, 2000.

Cunningham, Scott. *Cunningham's Encyclopedia of Magical Herbs*. St. Paul, MN: Llewellyn, 1985.

_____. *Magical Aromatherapy. The Power of Scent.* St. Paul, MN: Llewellyn, 1989.

Kloss, Jethro. *Back to Eden.* Loma Linda, CA. Back to Eden, 1939.

Mojay, Gabriel. *Aromatherapy for Healing the Spirit.* Rochester, VT: Healing Arts Press, 1997.

Pierson, PJ and Mary Shipley. *Aromatherapy for Everyone.* Garden City Park, NY: Square One Publishers, 2004.

Whitehurst, Tess. *Magical Housekeeping. Simple Charms and Practical Tips for Creating a Harmonious Home.* Woodbury, MN: Llewellyn, 2010.

Herbal Nervines

☙ by Calantirniel ☙

H erbs that possess a botanical property that is tonic, supportive, and healing to the nerves are referred to as "herbal nervines." Because of this, many nervines also help to alleviate pain and to bring calmness, and even be considered a relaxation and sleep aid. As you can imagine, these herbs are useful for nerve repair if there was damage. At least a hundred herbs could be categorized as a nervine—fifteen common nervines are presented here. A Preparation and Dosage Reference Guide can be found at the end of this article. Note: If you are pregnant, please seek the counsel of a knowledgeable practitioner.

Tonic Herbs

Black Cohosh (Cimicifuga racemosa)

Although most people automatically think of black cohosh root as a hormonal or menopausal herb, it has amazing healing qualities with nerves. It relieves pain, alleviates numbness and neuralgia, in a general sense. According to author and herbalist Matthew Wood, it generates fluids as well as unbinding them, providing nourishment to the nervous system and often pain relief, even for fibromyalgia or arthritis type of pain. In the past, it has also been a remedy for rattlesnake bite. It grows mostly in the eastern portion of the United States, but there is a plant that grows in the west called baneberry or red cohosh (*Actea arguta, A. rubra*) that has nearly identical healing properties, and apparently, there are similar plants across the pond. Caution: The berries are poisonous. Use only the roots of this plant.

Catnip (Nepeta cataria)

What would we do without catnip? One of my favorite nervine herbs from the mint family, it mixes well with some of the other herbs that do not taste as good and is safe for children. Catnip is a calming herb, making it useful for nervous tension, hyperactivity, and even insomnia. It is antispasmodic, making it a good one to add to headache remedies and to get relief from general pain that is due to spasms. It is excellent for colds and fever, since it can bring on a sweat. You can use catnip for skin irritations of nearly any type. Catnip is also used for digestive troubles, and is great for colic, constipation, and motion sickness. If you drink too much coffee and have the jitters, try a cup of catnip tea. As a bonus, your cats will love it, too.

Use the stems, leaves, and flowers either fresh or tinctured if possible.

Chamomile (Chamaemelum spp., Anthemis spp., Matricaria spp.)

Sometimes spelled camomile, this aromatic herb is one of the best "tummy trouble" herbs as it allows proper digestion. Like catnip, it is one of the better herbs for cranky children. For stress, it can calm nerves, and is a great sleep aid and pain reducer. Dr. Michael Tierra, author of *The Way of Herbs*, likes to combine chamomile with ginger for menstrual cramps. If it grows near you, you can also use pineapple weed (*Matricaria matricarioides*) in the same manner. Use the flowering tops, fresh or dried, and as a tincture for stronger medicinal use.

Cramp Bark (Viburnum trilobum, V. opulus)

While it is best known for uterine and menstrual cramps, due to its effectiveness, it can be implemented in many types of pain. At one time, the *US Pharmacopoeia* had it classified as a nervine sedative and antispasmodic useful for asthma and hysteria. Also called cranberry bush, which produces berries that are sour but edible, the medicinal aspect of cramp bark is actually in the inner layer of the bark. It is well worth including in your herbal arsenal.

Fennel (Foeniculum vulgare)

Known for its licorice-like flavor, the seeds are chewed to relieve gas and other digestive upsets. It is one of the best nervines for pain, and particularly with spasm. It can also be used to rid mucus and is a gentle reliever for constipation. It is also useful for combating colds and flu. Use whole dried seeds, and crush before making tea or tincture.

Hops (Humulus lupulus)

Hops are commonly known as the bitter-salty flavoring agent of beer, which could be one reason why people might crave a beer after a hard work day. Hops are wonderfully calming and sedative, and have diuretic and pain-relieving properties. It improves the appetite and promotes sleep, and can be used for stomach or liver disorder and, surprisingly, for cleansing the blood. Applied externally, it also relieves toothache, earache, and swelling from injury. Use fresh or dried female flowers (called strobiles, which look like cones), or tincture for stronger medicinal value.

Lemon Balm (Melissa officinalis)

One of the best-tasting nervine herbs in the mint family (making it excellent for children), lemon balm mixes well with many remedies for the digestive as well as the nervous system, ranging from nervous tension and insomnia to depression and melancholy. It is the very best internal and external remedy for herpes simplex (particularly as a warm poultice, alternated with an ice cube). It is also useful for combating fever. With all its calming properties, it can also bring on delayed menses and in smaller doses is useful for cramps. Use fresh or dried stems, leaves and/or flowers for tea, or tincture if stronger medicinal value is needed.

Linden Blossom (Tilia cordata)

In Europe, linden blossom (also called lime blossom) is consumed as a beverage tea, as is chamomile. It tastes good and, again, combines well with many of the herbs listed here and children will drink it (you can add a bit of raw honey or stevia). It can be used for colds and flus, and even menstrual cramps, so many people have this pleasant-tasting tea in their herbal collection.

Lobelia (Lobelia inflata)

Lobelia is a most unique herbal nervine. Dr. John Christopher, who founded of The School of Natural Healing and was student of old-time herbalists like Samuel Thompson, used it in nearly every blend. He explained that the herb stimulates healing and had "intelligence," which allowed the herbal formula to be accepted and quickly assimilated in the body. You likely will not want to have lobelia too dominant in a blend, because it can cause vomiting (and sometimes this can be a catalyst to wellness), but a small amount actually has the opposite effect (antiemetic). This herb is also an expectorant and can be used in the treatment of coughs, respiratory issues, and is even a specific for asthma. Called "Indian tobacco" by some, it can have tobacco-like effects without the addiction issue, and is a wonderful addition to mullein and other dried herbs for an herbal-smoking blend that is intended to help the user stop smoking tobacco. Use the stems, leaves, flowers, and seeds. A tincture in vinegar is especially effective medicinally; it can be tinctured in vodka, too.

Motherwort (Leonurus cardiaca)

This cool, bitter, spicy member of the mint family is a powerhouse favorite among the old-school female herbalists, who consider it one of the best heart tonics and circulatory aids available. Wise Woman Herbalist Susun Weed calls it a "bypass in a bottle." It is also an antispasmodic nervine herb that relieves nearly every type of pain, from an acute issue (toothache) to chronic conditions like CFS or fibromyalgia.

It is carminative, diuretic, and a very strong emmenogogue that stimulates blood flow in the uterus, where a longer-term use of the herb will eliminate menstrual cramps altogether. It is also used for nervousness, PMS, insomnia, hysteria, and convulsions/heart palpitations. It aids in the transition toward menopause (hot flashes, rapid heartbeat, vaginal moisture/ elasticity) and bolsters libido. Use fresh or dried stems, leaves and flowers; tincture in vinegar for nutritional/mineral long term use, or in 100-proof vodka for stronger medicinal value.

Mullein (Verbascum thapsus)

The healing herb mullein is so versatile. Known for its amazing ability to heal the lungs either internally or externally, it can also be dried and smoked, providing a mild base that is much better for lungs due to its demulcent/expectorant properties than tobacco or other substances. A common Dr. Christopher formula of ¾ mullein with ¼ lobelia is a formula you can use for any lymphatic or glandular problem. It will bring balance to glands, including but not limited to mammary glands, reproductive glands, and tonsils. It can heal wounds, too. It also combats diarrhea and has antispasmodic and pain relieving properties. Some herbalists use the root successfully with lower back pain due to injury. Mullein has slightly sedative and narcotic properties and, with its mild taste, combines well with other herbs. Use fresh or dried leaves and flowers or the first-year root in the autumn. To make oil for earaches, use olive oil with mullein flowers.

Passionflower (Passiflora incarnate)

Mild-tasting passionflower leaves are useful for treating Parkinson's, epilepsy, hysteria, shingles, whooping cough, asthma, hiccoughs, indigestion, vomiting, anxiety, hypertension, and neurological disorders, and it combines well with yarrow (*Achilles millefolium*). It is a hypnotic, antispasmodic, sedative and pain reliever that is used specifically to relax the cerebral area, calming an overactive mind that cannot "turn off." Use fresh or dried leaves, or tincture the fresh plant material for more medicinal value. (The fruit is a wonderful food.)

Scullcap (Scutellaria lateriflora)

A bitter nervine herb in the mint family, scullcap (also spelled skullcap) is a specific for rebuilding the central nervous system/spinal column. It works well with neurological diseases like epilepsy and chorea. It is even helpful for alcohol and drug withdrawal (particularly from sleeping pills), and even alone can eliminate hydrophobia. It works well for other pain when some herbs will not: sciatica, injury, headache, toothache, even ringing in the ears. And, like the others listed here, it relaxes nervous tension, creates calmness, and is good for insomnia. Use fresh stems, leaves, and flowers, or tincture immediately in vodka. When dried, it loses much of its medicinal potency.

Valerian (Valeriana spp.)

Why would anyone wish to use an herb that smells like unwashed feet? Because it is one of the most effective herbal pain relievers known. While it can be overbearing when used straight, if it is mixed with other pleasant-smelling/tasting nervines, and other strong and pleasant-tasting herbs for flavor (i.e., mints), valerian can be disguised fairly well. It is sedative, hypnotic, and amazing for treating insomnia, hysteria, stress, nervousness, menstrual cramps, spasm, gas relief, and pain. I may mention that if it is used as a sleep aid, you may not recall your dreams, but it is usually due to the body needing deep sleep, which valerian allows you to achieve. Use other herbs, like lemon balm, for dream-work. Use the root/ rhizome to obtain the most potent medicine (and potent-smelling), or if you have access to fresh stems, leaves and flowers, try them in an elixir—mix the fresh uppers with ⅓ raw honey and ⅔ brandy.

Wild Lettuce (Lactuga serriola, L. virosa)

Wild lettuce, also called prickly lettuce, is a bitter-tasting sedative nervine and is hypnotic, analgesic, gently laxative, expectorant, cough-suppressant, diuretic, and somewhat diaphoretic. Though it contains no opiates, it can act as a weak narcotic. This makes wild lettuce an often-overlooked sleep aid and excellent pain reliever, whether the pain is acute (as in gout or a headache) or chronic, as for fibromyalgia or chronic upper body tension. It is great for asthma as well as menstrual pain. It can be used externally to relieve sunburn pain and insect bites/stings. Use the stems, leaves, and flowers fresh, dried, or tinctured in vinegar or vodka.

This is only a mere sampling of nervines, and you may even think to yourself "Aren't there a few plants missing from this list? You are correct, and only because space in this article is not that plentiful. But I also wanted to introduce you to some herbs you may not have thought of using. Saint John's wort (*Hypericum spp.*) and white willow bark (*Salix alba*) do not work for everything, due to differing herbal action. The idea is to expand your herbal cabinet—especially if some of these plants grow near you. May you find peace and calm with your new plant allies!

Preparation and Dosage Reference Guide

Tea: Fresh Herb

If there is an immediate need, and the plant is available and in season, use the fresh plant parts specified to make a strong tea (also called an infusion). Just fill the teacup with plant material and pour boiling water over, cover, and steep for 10 to 15 minutes for leaves and flowers (20 minutes for roots and barks, also called a decoction). I like to squeeze the plant material to make sure most of the healing qualities are mixed into the tea. If needed, sweeten with raw honey, agave juice, stevia; or flavor with tamari sauce or liquid amino acids if you prefer a salty taste.

Tea: Dried Herb

When choosing herbs to dry for making tea infusions or decoctions, make sure they are at their peak and do not contain moisture. You can tie paper bags over the tops, then hang them upside-down away from the sun. If you have a wicker basket, they often dry nicely in one of those. Just keep the basket in a dry place and away from sunlight. If you live where humidity is high, placing it near the heat or air conditioning helps. Any bugs and dirt will fall away in the drying process. When thoroughly dry, place in a glass jar, away from sunlight. Use 1 teaspoon of crushed herbs for an 8-ounce cup of tea. Pour boiling water over the herbs, remove from heat source, and steep for 10 to 15 minutes (20 minutes for roots and barks).

Vinegar

Place as much of the fresh or dried herb into a glass jar as you can and fill the jar with raw apple cider vinegar (like Bragg's or Spectrum) up to the top. Seal and allow to sit in the fridge for about 6 to 8 weeks, shaking the contents periodically. Filter out the plant material with layered cheesecloth or even an unbleached coffee filter, and keep in the refrigerator. This is just as much food as it is medicine, and vinegar is particularly good for accessing the plant's minerals that are in a very accessible form. Ideal dose is 1 to 3 tablespoons per day, as a greens or salad dressing, or even straight and chased with water or tea. Especially important if you drink mineral-draining fluids like coffee, non-herbal tea, sodas, etcetera. These should be eliminated or used at a very bare minimum for maintaining and improving health.

Tincture

Collect fresh or dried plant material and fill a glass jar. Pour to the top either vodka or brandy (40- to 50-percent alcohol). Seal and allow to sit for about 6 to 8 weeks, shaking the jar every now and then to assist the further extraction of medicinal properties of the herb. Filter plant material out with layered cheesecloth or an unbleached coffee filter, and keep in a dark dry place. These are not foods, but are wonderful medicines. They store nearly indefinitely and you can use when needed for a condition 6 days a week, taking a break the seventh day. Dosage can be 15 to 30 drops 2 to 3 times a day, or more if needed, and can be used until the condition improves or leaves, which can be many months.

Oil

Collect fresh plant material, and allow to slightly wilt, to remove excess water content, or use dried plant material, before filling a glass jar. Pour to the top cold-pressed olive oil, grapeseed oil, apricot kernel oil, or other non-processed vegetable-based oil. Seal with a rubber band and a few layers of cheesecloth (or other breathable material, especially if fresh to allow moisture to leave) and allow to sit out of the sunlight for about 6 to 8 weeks, stirring periodically. Filter through an unbleached coffee filter (this takes awhile and can be messy). Oil is best used with external applications.

Liniment

For external use. Combine one-half of a filtered herbal oil and one-half of a filtered vinegar or tincture, or at a proportion you like. Shake well before applying to affected areas.

Poultice/Fomentation

For external use. Break down fresh plant material (chewing works well in a pinch), moisten fresh or dried herbs with warm water and apply the herbs (poultice) directly to the affected area. Cover with a paper towel or warmed cloth. Or wet a cloth with prepared infusion/decoction (fomentation) and apply to the affected area.

Resources

Christopher, Dr. John R. *School of Natural Healing* (25th anniversary edition). Springville, UT: Christopher Publications, 2001.

Tierra, Michael. *The Way of Herbs*. New York: Pocket Books/ Simon & Schuster, 1998.

Tilford, Gregory L. *Edible and Medicinal Plants of the West*, Missoula, MT: Mountain Press Publishing Company, 1997.

Wood, Matthew. *The Earthwise Herbal, A Complete Guide to Old World Medicinal Plants*. Berkeley, CA: North Atlantic Books, 2008.

Wood, Matthew. *The Earthwise Herbal, A Complete Guide to New World Medicinal Plants*. Berkeley, CA: North Atlantic Books, 2009.

Internet Resources

Many herbal resources can be found online here: http://aartiana.wordpress.com/herbalism/

Herb Soups that Heal

❧ by Darcey Blue French ❧

Your granny always knew that a steaming bowl of chicken soup was the best medicine when you felt sick. Long before herbs came in capsules, or even herbal tinctures, people all over the world used herbs in teas and soups to make medicines. Though tinctures and capsules are certainly convenient, many herbs used for healing lend themselves better to long cooking in tea or soup.

The benefits of soup itself are numerous. The best broths are made by cooking animal bones (chicken, beef, lamb, or others) in a large amount of water with a source of acid, usually lemon or vinegar, for a long period of time. These "bone broths" are full

of minerals, including calcium, magnesium, phosphorus, and potassium, as well as collagen and gelatin.

Not only are the minerals contained in bone broths important for bones, they are vital to the healthy function of muscles, nervous system, and every cell in the body. Collagen and gelatin are known to improve the elasticity of skin and strengthen hair and nails; they also repair and maintain a healthy digestive tract. Bone broth is considered by many natural health practitioners as one of the most nourishing healing foods available to us, in a time when many of our foods are lacking in minerals and vitamins resulting from depleted soils or excessive processing. Of course, you want to make sure to use bones from organically raised, and if possible, pastured grass-fed animals to avoid antibiotics, hormones, and other toxins associated with industrial meat production.

Basic Bone Broth

1 pound bones from organic, free-range
chicken, beef, lamb, shellfish, or fish

2 cups cold water, or enough to cover the bones

1 tablespoon vinegar or lemon juice

1. Add all the ingredients to a large stock pot or crock pot.

2. Bring to a low simmer.

3. Cover and cook on very low heat at least 8 hours, but up to 36. The longer it cooks the better it gets!

4. Periodically check the level of the liquid and replenish to keep the bones covered. A crockpot can easily be left on "low" for a few days at a time. If you are using a stockpot on the stove, you may turn it off when leaving the house

or sleeping, but make sure to bring it to a simmer and reduce the heat again when you return to cooking.

5. After the cooking, remove from heat and cool. Strain bones from the liquid and store in portion sized jars or freezer bags. Broth keeps for a week in the refrigerator. Freeze for longer storage.

Adding Healing Herbs

The addition of herbs to this healing broth can make a remarkable medicine. I've included some recipes to start with, but once you get the hang of it, you can create your own healing soup brews by choosing herbs that you like and are appropriate for the situation at hand. Here is a brief introduction to some of the most commonly used soup herbs.

Astragalus Root

The Chinese say that astragalus strengthens the "wei-qi" or the shield qi. Think of your immune system as a shield that protects you, and astragalus makes it stronger. This herb is safe for all ages and tastes mild and sweet. It works best when taken regularly over a long period of time, and it should not be used during acute illness.

Burdock

Burdock is known as gobo in Japan and is used frequently in stir fries and as a pickle. In the West, burdock is best known as a blood cleanser and liver ally. It helps the liver produce bile, and is rich in inulin, a starch that feeds the friendly flora that colonize the digestive tract. Many people reach for burdock when they have skin problems that stem from a sluggish liver. Burdock is sweet and bitter.

Calendula

Calendula, or pot marigold, is primarily used as a skin healing remedy, but has many other traditional uses as well. It assists the lymph fluid in flowing freely through the body, which improves general immunity. It is a very important remedy, used internally, for anyone with inflammatory digestive problems. It can also heal the tissues in the digestive tract just as well as on the skin. The dried petals have traditionally been added to soups throughout history, and bring a measure of bright sunshine to every meal during dark winter months.

Dandelion

Dandelion—reviled weed, glorified medicinal herb, and food —grows up through the concrete wherever it can. It is a superb soup herb! Dandelion is known as a liver and kidney ally. It also aids in digestion through its bitter taste and by supporting healthy liver function. It is full of minerals such as calcium, magnesium, potassium, and iron.

Ginger

Most people are familiar with ginger tea. It stimulates healthy digestion, improves circulation, quells nausea and gas, and is an anti-inflammatory. Fresh ginger is milder in flavor than dried ginger, and either is fine to use in soups. Ginger will provide a warming, stimulating effect that carries the benefits of other herbs and nutrients to all parts of the body.

Kelp

Kelp is just one kind of seaweed available to us. It is full of minerals like calcium and magnesium, and a rich mucilage that coats and lubricates tissues and joints. You can use other seaweeds as you desire, but I find that kelp's bigger pieces are easier to cook with and remove.

Licorice Root

Licorice root is the great harmonizer of traditional Chinese medicine, and is included in many Chinese remedies to bring balance to the formula. Licorice has a very sweet taste, and can be included in soup broths in small amounts. It nourishes the adrenal glands, balances various hormones throughout the endocrine system, is anti-inflammatory, heals and soothes the tissues of the digestive tract, and supports the lungs as an expectorant and demulcent. Many have found licorice root to be helpful for acid reflux and dry, irritated coughs. Note that licorice root contains compounds that can cause some people to retain water and increase blood pressure. Do not use licorice if you have high blood pressure or take steroidal anti-inflammatory medications.

Medicinal Mushrooms

There are many mushrooms that fall into this category. Each is unique, and all of them are supreme immune system allies. They strengthen a weak immune system, balance an overactive immune system, and act on all the systems on the body to restore balance and well-being. Reishi has been used by emperors in China for more than 4,000 years as a health tonic. It is a woody and bitter-tasting mushroom that is inedible, but when cooked for long periods of time, the resulting broth provides all the benefits. Tastier shitake mushrooms can be cooked into soups and eaten right out of the broth. Other beneficial medicinal mushrooms include chaga, turkey tails,

maitake, and cordyceps. All are beneficial additions to medicinal soups.

Nettle

Stinging nettles are the nutritional powerhouse of the herb
kingdom. One of the most nutritionally dense land plants
available to us, it is loaded with iron, calcium, magnesium, potassium, and vitamins A, C, and K. Nettles enrich the blood,
support good kidney and adrenal health, and build strong
bones, nails, teeth, and hair.

Schisandra

Schisandra is another Chinese herb with a long tradition of
use in soups. It is called the five-flavored fruit, because it contains all five tastes: sweet, salty, sour, bitter, and pungent. The
Chinese have used this fruit to strengthen the lungs, the kidneys and adrenal glands, the immune system, and to protect
the liver.

Turmeric

Turmeric is closely related to ginger and is less pungent in
flavor, but is exceedingly beneficial as an anti-inflammatory
and antioxidant. It stimulates, cleanses, and protects the liver;
it reduces the pain of inflammatory conditions like arthritis,
stimulates tissue healing and the immune system. Used in
soups, it also improves the appetite and digestive function.

Immune Soup

This soup is ideal to enjoy during the cold winter months
when you want extra support for your immune system. The
herbs in this recipe are tonic herbs, meaning they work best

taken over long periods of time to build your natural resistance to illness and improve immune function. The broth may be slightly bitter from the herbs; use salt to taste. Take 8 ounces broth 3 to 5 times per week. Use this broth as a base for soups, to cook grains, or sip a cup warm with breakfast or lunch.

Ingredients:

3 quarts water

1 pounds cracked chicken or beef marrow bones

1 tablespoon lemon juice or vinegar

1 onion, quartered

6 cloves garlic, sliced

1 cup astragalus root sticks (milk vetch)

¼ cup schisandra berries (magnolia vine)

½ cup elderberries

¼ cup reishi mushroom slices

⅓ cup calendula blossoms

8 shitake mushrooms, fresh or dried

2 teaspoons sea salt

1 teaspoon black peppercorns, cracked

½ teaspoon cayenne pepper (optional)

Directions:

1. Crack bones to expose marrow. A nutcracker or mallet works well.

2. In large stock pot, add fresh water, lemon juice or vinegar, and bones. Bring to a simmer.

3. Reduce heat and add the remaining ingredients. Stir to mix and cover and simmer over very low heat for 8 to

12 hours, covered. Check water level periodically, and add a cup of water to cover the bones if needed.

5. Remove from heat and cool.

Spring Cleaning Soup

This spring soup is the perfect way to reinvigorate and strengthen the body's natural detoxification systems in spring time. Take up to 2 cups of broth 3 to 5 times per week during the spring or daily when on an elimination/cleansing diet. Use this broth as a base for soups, to cook grains, or sip a cup warm with breakfast or lunch.

Ingredients:

3 quarts water

1 pound cracked chicken or beef marrow bones

1 tablespoon lemon juice or vinegar

1 onion quartered

4 cloves garlic

1 cup burdock root (fresh sliced or dried)

¼ to ½ cup dandelion roots (fresh or dried)

1 cup dried or fresh nettle leaf

1 cup chopped parsley leaf

2 teaspoons turmeric powder

½ to 1 teaspoon cayenne

1 or 2 strips kelp seaweed

2 teaspoons sea salt

2 teaspoons black peppercorns, cracked

Miso paste, green onion, cilantro, or chopped almonds for garnish

Directions:

1. Crack bones to expose marrow. A nutcracker or mallet works well.

2. In large stock pot, add fresh water, lemon juice or vinegar, and bones. Bring to a simmer.

3. Reduce heat and add the herbs, onion, garlic, salt, and pepper. Stir to mix and cover.

4. Cover and simmer over very low heat for 8 to 12 hours. Check water level periodically, and add a cup of water to cover the bones if needed.

5. Remove from heat and cool.

6. Garnish with green onion, cilantro, or chopped almonds, or stir in miso paste.

Cold and Flu Soup

Make this soup specifically when you are feeling unwell or coming down with a cold. It will help to address the cough, sniffles, stuffy head, chest congestion, and sneezes. Consume liberally. Sip this broth hot throughout the day when you have a cold.

Ingredients:

3 quarts water

1 pound cracked chicken or beef marrow bones

1 tablespoon lemon juice or vinegar

1 onion quartered

6 cloves garlic

2 tablespoons fresh ginger root, grated

½ cup chopped fresh basil

1 tablespoon fresh sage leaf

1 tablespoon fresh thyme leaf

½ cup marshmallow root

1 teaspoon cayenne

3 teaspoons salt

2 teaspoons black peppercorns, cracked

1. Crack bones to expose marrow. A nutcracker or mallet works well.

2. In large stock pot, add fresh water, lemon juice or vinegar, and bones. Bring to a simmer.

3. Simmer on very low for 8 to 12 hours, covered. Check water level periodically, and add a cup of water to cover the bones if needed.

4. Add the herbs, onion, garlic, salt, and pepper. Stir to mix and cover.

5. Simmer for 20 to 30 minutes.

6. Remove from heat and cool.

Herbal Remedies for Hot Lungs

✺ by Sean Donahue ✺

I f you ask any good clinical herb-alist: "What herbs are good for the lungs?" or "What herbs are good for a chest cold?" she is likely to answer, "It depends . . ." Then she will begin asking a lot of detailed questions about the specific situation.

This is not an attempt to be eva-sive or to hold on tight to secrets of the trade. It's just that an herbalist uses herbs differently than a doctor uses pharmaceuticals. Pharmaceu-ticals work to stimulate or repress particular chemical processes in the body or to kill particular viruses, bacteria, or fungi. Herbs can be used this way, but they work best when they are used to help the body help itself correct imbalances.

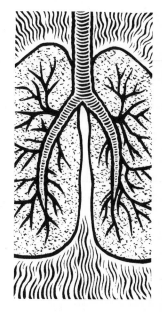

Traditional Western herbalism tends to look at balances of heat and cold and moisture and dryness in identifying and correcting imbalances. And it's entirely possible, and even common, for the same disease to cause a different pattern of imbalances in different people depending on environmental factors and constitutional factors (our bodies' predispositions to certain kinds of imbalances). For example, the person who is usually sweating when everyone else is cold is probably more prone to "hot" inflammatory conditions than the person who starts reaching for a sweater when the temperature drops below 75°F.)

Just like people, each herb has its own tendencies to be cooling or relaxing, moistening or drying, toning or relaxing. (Though some herbs will adjust an organ or a system or the whole body in whichever direction it needs to shift—these herbs are "amphoteric.") Generally speaking, we use herbs that are the energetic opposite of the problem we are trying to correct. For example, if someone's tissues are too dried out, we'll use herbs that moisten the tissues.

It takes a lot of study and practice to get really familiar with the energetics of people and herbs. And if you have a serious or chronic respiratory condition, I strongly suggest working with an experienced clinician. But there are some basic guidelines you can follow in helping yourself or someone you love heal from a mild to moderate respiratory infection by identifying whether their respiratory system is experiencing too much heat or too much cold, too much moisture or too much dryness.

If you are pregnant or dealing with a chronic health condition, consult a health-care practitioner before using any of these herbs.

Hot Respiratory Conditions

Both bacterial and viral infections often begin with inflammation of the respiratory tract. Allergies can also produce respiratory inflammation.

The tissues become red, hot, tender, and irritated. Often the sick person's cheeks will begin to turn red. The tip of the tongue, which is associated with the heart and lungs in Chinese tongue diagnosis, will appear red as well.

The inflammatory response is the first wave of the body's immune response. But in excess it can prevent healthy tissue function.

Treatment in a hot respiratory condition often begins with the use of herbs that help to cool the tissues down by slowing the oxidation response at the cellular level. Peach and cherry are two favorites here.

Wild Cherry

Wild cherry (*Prunus virginica*) bark has traditionally been used for respiratory conditions where a person's cheeks turn cherry red. In addition to being profoundly cooling, wild cherry bark is relaxing to the point of being sedative. It also suppresses the cough reflex. This can allow for sleep where a hacking cough is keeping someone awake. But it is to be used with great care when there is significant fluid buildup in the lungs. I will sometimes use wild cherry at night to allow for sleep and then use an expectorant herb in the morning to bring up the phlegm. (We will talk about expectorants in a bit.)

Adult dose of the tincture is 10 drops every 4 hours. To get the appropriate dose of most herbs for a child you can divide the child's weight in pounds by 150 to get the right fraction of the adult dose. (So a 50-pound child would take 3 drops of wild cherry bark tincture every 4 hours.)

Wild cherry bark syrups are popular, but I tend to avoid them since most contain sugar and sugar suppresses healthy immune response. Honey-based syrups are okay, though, because honey has its own antimicrobial actions and also helps to soothe the throat.

Peach

Peach (*Prunus persica*) is commonly used in Southern folk-medicine. The great Appalachian herbalist Tommie Bass said that peach bark was most effective, but I've primarily worked with peach leaf, which works great as either a tincture or a tea. Peach leaf is very gentle and is suitable for children. It is great for cooling overheated lungs and also helps to soothe heat in the digestive tract, which makes it ideal in flus that have both respiratory and intestinal symptoms. And because peach doesn't suppress the cough reflex, it's useful in cases where you want to allow coughing to continue in order to clear out excess mucus from the lungs.

Peach leaves and bark aren't widely commercially available, so it's great to gather your own. The ideal time is before the trees blossom, but as long as the leaves have a bitter almond flavor they will be effective.

Adult dosage: 1 to 10 drops of the bark tincture or 10 to 30 drops of the leaf tincture. Peach leaf tea is delicious and can be given liberally.

Fight a Fever

Fever also often accompanies respiratory inflammation. This is part of the natural immune response, and a fever stemming from an infection will never rise to a truly dangerous level. But fever can cause discomfort that prevents healing rest.

Suppressing a fever with aspirin or acetaminophen or even fever suppressant herbs can compromise immune response and prolong infection. So as herbalists, we tend to work to support the body's natural means of cooling itself down by using herbs called diaphoretics. Stimulating diaphoretics move blood from the core of the body to the surface to cool it down. Relaxing diaphoretics relax the skin to open the pores and let heat escape.

Two diaphoretics can be especially helpful in hot respiratory conditions.

Elder Flower

Elder flower (*Sambucus candensis, Sambucus nigra*), as a lot of people know, has similar antiviral properties to elder berries. A compound in elder berries helps to stop viral reproduction, and taken in frequent large doses, I've seen elder berries help cut the duration of a viral infection roughly in half. Less known, but equally wonderful, however, is the medicine of elder flowers.

Elder flowers are soothing, act directly to cool the respiratory tract, and are also a great relaxing diaphoretic. Deb Soule of Avena Botanicals points out that the elder flower is shaped like a eustachian tube, making it a perfect medicine for respiratory conditions that result in earaches.

I like to give elder flowers as a tea, both because the tea is delicious, and because its a great way of getting fluids into the body. Serve the tea hot and sip slowly throughout the day, reheating as needed.

Butterfly Weed

Butterfly weed (*Asclepias tuberosa*) is also known as pleurisy root. Pleurisy is the inflammation of the lining of the lungs, and this member of the milkweed family is the classic remedy for pleurisy. Give it when the skin is hot and dry, the person is tense, and there is pain with breathing and coughing. Butterfly weed will soothe the inflamed tissues and is also a relaxing diaphoretic.

In addition, butterfly weed has an amazing gift for regulating fluid levels in the lungs—it will help whether the lungs are too wet or too dry. Michigan herbalist Jim McDonald points out that it is especially helpful when the upper respiratory tract is dry but there is fluid deep in the lungs that you can't cough out.

Put 2 to 3 droppers full of the tincture into a cup of hot water and sip slowly over the course of a half an hour. Give it up to 3 times a day.

You can also put butterfly weed roots and elder flowers in an old sock, tie it up, and throw it in a lukewarm bath.

Cold Respiratory Conditions

When a respiratory infection lingers, it cools and moves deeper into the lungs. The cheeks become pale. The person may become listless.

The warming, aromatic kitchen herbs—thyme, basil, oregano, sage—are all great here. Use them in food, make teas, simmer them in a pot of water and have the person breathe in the steam, put them in an old sock and throw it in a hot bath. Garlic and onions will help too.

This is also a great time to make a traditional mustard plaster—mix dried mustard with clay or flour, add water to make a paste, and plaster it across the chest.

Essential oils of eucalyptus, pine, cedar, frankincense, and myrrh are worth a try. Dilute them in water or a carrier oil before applying to the chest.

Ideally, with this kind of persistent infection you should consult a clinical herbalist.

Dry Respiratory Conditions

The lungs depend on the correct amount of moisture to function well. Prolonged inflammation dries out the mucosa, impairing respiratory function. A dry, unproductive cough is the first and clearest sign here, often accompanied by a sore throat. Dry lips and tongue and dark, scanty urine are further indicators—the latter suggesting that the dryness is becoming more systemic.

The herbs that I reach for first are herbs like marsh mallow and slippery elm that are high in polysaccharides that are sweet, bland, and form a mucilage that directly coats the effected tissue. Most of these herbs tend to be slightly cooling.

Polysaccharides extract best in water. To get the most out of demulcent herbs, its best to give them plenty of time to get good and slimy—so overnight cold water infusions are ideal. Put a handful of the herb into a jar of water, cover and leave overnight. Add 5 to 15 drops of butterfly weed tincture. Sip throughout the day.

Marsh Mallow

Marsh mallow (*Althea officinalis*) is my favorite herb for dry coughs. Marsh mallow helps to moisten all of the mucous membranes, and is also soothing and anti-inflammatory. Because it's also salty, it works to some degree with the kidneys, regulating moisture through the body. The root is most effective and most widely available, but the leaves will do in a pinch.

Slippery Elm

Slippery elm (*Ulmus rubra*) bark is not as powerfully anti-inflammatory as marsh mallow, but is wonderfully soothing and moistening. I tend to use it more in treating digestive issues, but it has a long history of use for dry respiratory conditions.

The popularity of slippery elm has put wild populations of the tree at risk. Its cousin, Siberian elm (*Ulmus pumila*) is almost identical in its medicinal actions, and is a highly invasive "weed tree" that is overrunning pastures and fields in the Midwest and the Northeast. Siberian elm bark is not widely available, but if you live in one of these regions and want to make your own medicine, you should have no trouble finding a suitable Siberian elm from which to harvest it.

In hot, dry lung conditions, the mucus often becomes thick and sticky, coating tissues. Salty herbs can help to break it up, loosening from the bronchi and lungs.

Mullein

Mullein (*Verbascum thaspus*) is one of the first herbs to grow after a forest fire, and it is the premier respiratory herb for "burned over" respiratory tissues.

Mullein is a great expectorant which also soothes the underlying tissues where they have become irritated. Energetically, it has a strong but gentle upward motion. But it also is relaxing to muscular tissue and hence helps to open the lungs and larynx allowing for deeper breath. And it helps to calm violent spasmodic coughs, allowing them to give way to gentler and more productive coughs.

In addition, mullein is a great lymphatic herb, so it can help the body to clear the waste that builds up during a prolonged infection.

Tea or tincture are both effective, though I tend to go with mullein teas, because in cases where mullein is indicated, the body generally needs more fluids.

Excess moisture can be as serious a problem for the lungs as excess dryness. The tissues normally secrete mucus both to moisten the lungs and to remove waste products. Infection or irritation can lead to the overproduction of mucus which thickens into phlegm and becomes stuck in the lungs and bronchi, obstructing breath,

Wheezing and a damp cough will be typical symptoms, though sometimes there is a shallow, dry cough when the body can't muster the strength for the kind of deep cough that can bring the phlegm up and out. Look for thick, frothy saliva streaming from the edges of the tongue.

The immediate need here is to clear the obstruction. One of the clearest and simplest ways to do this is through herbs that stimulate a deep, healthy cough. Among my favorites are:

Elecampane

Elecampane (*Inula helenium*) is a bright yellow, resinous flower that grows over six feet tall with a deep root with a bitter but tangy flavor. A tincture or tea of the root will work both to dry the secretions and to promote a healthy, deep cough to bring the phlegm up and out. For acute conditions, I use 30 to 60 drops of tincture 4 to 6 times a day. I tend to prefer the tincture of the fresh root because I feel like it helps to hold on to the volatile oils of the root which are responsible for much of its expectorant action. Honey can be a really nice way to preserve the roots as well.

Elecampane also has some antibacterial action—so is indicated when phlegm is thick and green or yellow. In addition, it is high in inulin, an indigestible starch that feeds the gut flora, helping to maintain healthy gut ecology. So it is indicated where food allergies cause the gut to back up, leading to bacterial infections that in turn back up into the respiratory tract. In these cases, elecamapne may also have a mild stimulating effect on the liver, aiding in its clearance.

Herbalist and founder of Sunnyfield Herb Farm Matthew Wood says that elecampane is helpful when "the cough cannot descend deep enough to bring up the mucus; afterward the mucus gushes out, is swallowed, and causes indigestion." The first herb I reach for in dealing with wet lung conditions is osha (*Ligusticum porteri*). Osha is strongly expectorant and also helps to open the airways and to strengthen the lungs themselves (hence its great benefit for those having trouble breathing at the high altitudes where it grows). It also has some antimicrobial properties that may aid in dealing with any deep, lingering infections. It helps to carry other herbs deep into the lungs as well. Use 20 to 60 drops of tincture up to 4 times a day. Osha is an endangered plant, so use it sparingly, and make sure you are buying from an ecologically responsible company.

Eastern Skunk Cabbage

Eastern skunk cabbage (*Symplocarpus foetidus*): In my mind this is one of the great forgotten medicines for old, persistent, stagnant lung conditions. Skunk cabbage grows in swamps, so is ideal for boggy lungs. It helps to bring up phlegm from deep in the lungs. I think of it as a plant that "gets the waters moving." It is a very stimulating expectorant, but it is also antispasmodic, so it will encourage a deep, productive cough, but prevent the cough from becoming an uncontrollable spasm.

Skunk cabbage is the first plant up in the spring—so I associate it with winter lung infections that have lingered on into early spring. It has thermogenic roots that melt the ice around it. I harvest it in March when the flower is still green (not yet purple). The root has oxalate crystals that can be excessively irritating, so I dry the root before tincturing it. This is a plant used in relatively low doses—5 to 10 drops at a time 4 times a day.

Western skunk cabbage is a plant of the same family but a different genus and has somewhat similar medicinal actions.

All of these herbs are somewhat warming, so if you are dealing with a hot, wet condition use them in combination with cooling herbs—and use more of the cooling herb than of the expectorant. Surprisingly, marsh mallow and slippery elm can be really helpful in wet lung conditions, because they make the mucus slipperier and easier to move.

Butterfly weed is a great herb to use in conjunction with these expectorants as well.

Shoo Fly

by Elizabeth Barrette

P ests can make life miserable, and so can repellents if you're not careful. Most modern repellents consist of harsh chemicals that can cause problems for pets and people, especially pregnant women or children. Fortunately, alternatives do exist. Plants have been fending off pests for millions of years. They've gotten quite good at it, and you can borrow their expertise.

People have tried many ways to get rid of pests. Probably the earliest involved rubbing the body with herbs; examples included mint, rue, and wormwood. When people began building houses, many cultures used strewing herbs added to the rushes or mats that covered the floors; popular choices were lavender, pennyroyal, and tansy. Clothing gained protection via fragrant leaves or woods such as bay leaves, cypress wood, or cedar wood. Smudges, incenses, and other fumigants were burned; these included fleabane, galbanum, sage, and willow. Pesticide sprays were also made from highly poisonous plants such as monkshood and oleander.

Note that these examples varied from one place to another. Different plants tend to repel different pests, although some plants affect a very wide range of offenders. Learn which plants are native to your area and which imported varieties grow well there. Also study your local pests. You may find that local plants are adapted to discourage local pests better than plants from elsewhere.

Repellent Herbs

Plants repel or kill pests through chemical warfare. Therefore, seek herbs with a strong fragrance. Some smell pleasant to humans but not pests, while others just plain stink. Here are some popular and effective repellant herbs to get you started.

Cedar

Cedar (*Cedurs atlantica*) repels ants, fleas, leeches, mice, mosquitoes, moths, rats, and woodworms. Active components include cedrol, sequiterpenes, and terpenic hydrocarbons. Store items in wooden containers or use essential oil in repellent blends.

Chrysanthemum

Chrysanthemum (*Chrysanthemum cinerariaefolium* or *C. roseum*) repels or kills ants, bedbugs, cockroaches, flies, mice, mites, mosquitoes, and moths. Make a spray to protect garden plants. Grow in the garden or near doorways to deter insects.

These plants contain pyrethrins that are among the stronger active components, and they affect beneficial insects as well as harmful ones. Use as a last resort and spray carefully.

Feverfew

Feverfew (*Tanacetum parthenium*) repels bees, flies, gnats, and mosquitoes. Active components include sesquiterpene lactones (such as parthenolide and santamarine) and tannins. Brew a strong tea, spray on skin, and allow to dry.

Garlic

Garlic (*Allium sativum*) repels aphids, mealy bugs, slugs, snails, and other sucking/chewing pests on plants; also discourages fungal growth. Repels fleas, mosquitoes, ticks, and other biting pests on humans and pets. Repels cockroaches, gnats, horn flies, house flies, fire ants, no-see-ums, and stable flies in buildings. Discourages deer, mice, rats, squirrels, and some other mammals from bothering your garden. Active components include allicin, citral, geraniol, and phellandrene. Garlic can be made into a spray or paste and applied to items or areas to be protected. It can also be eaten or taken as supplement pills to discourage biting pests.

German Chamomile

German Chamomile (*Matricaria recutita*) repels flies and mosquitoes. Make a very strong tea and spray to discourage pests. Applied to plants, chamomile tea also helps to prevent mildew, damping off, and other fungal infections. Active components include bisbolol, chamazulene, farnesense, and flavonoids. Unlike many repellants, chamomile is soothing and even features anti-inflammatory properties.

Lavender

Lavender (*Lavandul*, especially *L. angustifolia*) repels ants, fleas, flies, lice, moths, mosquitoes, and silverfish. Active components include camphor, cineole, borneol, flavonoids, lavendulyl acetate, limonene, pinene, tannins, terpinenol, triterpenoids. Use in crafts such as lavender wands, sachets, or powders. Add essential oil or florets to repellent blends.

Lemon Grass

Lemon grass (*Cymbopogon citrates*) repels ants, flies, gnats, mosquitoes, and ticks. It is also said to discourage snakes in the garden. Active components include citral, citronellol, dipentene, geraniol, and limonene. Rub leaves on skin to deter mosquitoes. Ground dried leaves may be used in powders. Essential oil is a good mosquito and flea repellent in blends.

Mint

Mint (*Mentha*, especially *M. piperita* and *M. spicata*) repels ants, aphids, chiggers, fleas, flies, mice, moths, rats, ticks, and wasps. Active components include azulenes, betaine, bisabolene, cineole, flavonoids, isomenthol, limonene, neomenthol, menthol, menthone, menthofuran, menthylacetate, pulegone, and tocopherols. Use mint water or tea as a spray. Add essential oil or powdered leaves to repellent blends. Place essential oil on cottonballs to plug entrances used by ants or other crawling insects.

Neem

Neem (*Azadirachta indica*) repels or disables hundreds of pests, including aphids, beetles, centipedes, cockroaches, fleas, flies, grasshoppers, millipedes, mites, moths, termites, thrips, and weevils. It also has antifungal and antibacterial qualities. Neem contains over 25 active components, including azadirachtin, its key pest control. Neem oil appears in many natural pest control products.

Pennyroyal

Pennyroyal (*Mentha pulegium*) repels or kills ants, aphids, cabbage maggots, chiggers, fleas, flies, gadflies, gnats, mosquitoes, and ticks. May discourage birds and mammals from bothering plants or equipment. Active components include isomenthone, isopulegone, limonene, menthol, neomenthol, piperitone, and pulegone. Grow in the garden or near doorways to deter pests. Add essential oil or dried leaves to repellent blends. Note: Pregnant women should avoid pennyroyal, as it can cause miscarriage.

Rue

Rue (*Ruta graveolens*) repels ants, fleas, and Japanese beetles. It also discourages cats, dogs, and other mammals from bothering your herb garden. Active components include alkaloids, glycosides, flavonoids, methyl-nonyl-ketone, and methyl-heptyl-ketone. Use the leaves to make a spray or add essential oil to repellent blends.

Note: Rue is particularly allergenic and also makes skin more susceptible to sunburn. For maximum safety, don't use on people.

Santolina

Santoina (*Santolina chamaecyparissus*) repels fleas, flies, moths, and silverfish. Active components include kinetin and luteolin. This herb, sometimes called "lavender cotton," blends well with English lavender in sachets or powders.

Tansy

Tansy (*Tanacetum vulgare*) repels or kills ants, bedbugs, cabbage worms, cockroaches, Colorado potato beetles, flea beetles, flies, Japanese beetles, mice, mites, mosquitoes, moths, squash bugs, and striped cucumber beetles. Active components include bornyl acetate, camphor, flavonoids, sesquiterpene lactones, thujone, and umbellulone. Grow near doorways or in gardens to discourage pests. Add dried leaves to powders or other repellent blends. Note: Pregnant women should avoid tansy, as it can cause miscarriage.

Wormwood

Wormwood (*Artemesia absinthium*) repels or kills aphids, caterpillars, codling moths, fleas, flies, lice, mice, mites, moths, rats, slugs, and white flies. Active compounds include absinthum, chamazulene, pinene, tannins, and thujone. Grow in the garden or near doorways to discourage pests. Add essential oil or powdered leaves to repellent blends.

Make Your Own Repellents

As mentioned above, most herbs that repel or kill pests work fine alone. However, by combining different ingredients you can make a stronger repellent that deters more types of pest. You can also choose various forms of repellent that target specific uses. The following crafts are samples—you can adapt these basic ideas to your particular needs.

Safety Tips

Remember that not everyone responds the same way to herbs; always test body products on a small patch of skin and wait a day before using larger amounts. For garden and other products, wear gloves while working with them, try to avoid direct contact, and wash your hands after you finish. Ideally, use an enamel pan when heating herbs, and do not use the same pan for herbal crafts that you use for cooking food.

Bug Spray

> 2 cups water
>
> 2 teaspoons dried chamomile
>
> 2 teaspoons dried feverfew
>
> 3 teaspoons dried mint
>
> Peel of 1 lemon
>
> Peel of 1 orange
>
> 2 cups rubbing alcohol

1. Put 2 cups water in a pot. Add dried chamomile, dried feverfew, dried mint, lemon peel, and orange peel. Heat water until it just starts to boil, then remove from heat. Allow the tea to steep overnight.

2. Pour the tea through cheesecloth to strain out all the herbs. Put the tea into a spray bottle.

3. Add 2 cups alcohol. Cap the spray bottle very tightly to prevent the alcohol from evaporating, and shake to combine.

To use, spray on skin or clothing and allow to dry, or use as an air spray. Repels ants, bees, chiggers, flies, gnats, mosquitoes, ticks, and wasps.

Essential Oil Bug Repellent

8 ounces light carrier oil (such as apricot, sunflower, or grapeseed oil)

20 drops citronella oil

10 drops lavender oil

7 drops mint oil

5 drops neem oil

3 drops garlic oil

1. Pour light carrier oil into a flip-top squeeze bottle. Add essential oils. Cap tightly and shake to combine.

2. Allow the oils to marry overnight before use.

3. Store away from light.

To use, squirt a small amount of oil onto skin and rub it in. You can also put some oil on a cotton ball or rag and attach it to your shoes, hat, hair, etc., if you don't want oil directly on your skin. However, be careful, because then it can stain clothing. Repels ants, beetles, centipedes, chiggers, fleas, flies, gnats, lice, millipedes, mites, mosquitoes, no-see-ums, ticks, and wasps.

Garden Spray

1 quart water

3 tablespoons fresh chamomile

3 tablespoons fresh feverfew

3 tablespoons fresh chrysanthemum, optional

1 tablespoon fresh pennyroyal

1 tablespoon fresh rue

1 tablespoon fresh tansy

1 tablespoon fresh wormwood

1 whole garlic bulb

½ teaspoon neem oil

1. Fill a pot with 1 quart water. Add fresh herbs.

2. Heat until the water starts to boil, then remove from heat.

3. Dice or crush one whole garlic bulb and add that to the liquid.

4. Allow to steep overnight.

5. Pour the liquid through a strainer to remove the herb bits.

6. Put the liquid into a large spray bottle. Add neem oil and shake well to blend.

Always shake before using. Spray onto plants, covering both sides of the leaves. (Don't spray while direct sunlight shines on the leaves, as that can cause sunburn. Repels or disables many pests, including aphids, cabbage maggots, cabbage worms, caterpillars, Colorado potato beetles, flea beetles, Japanese beetles, grasshoppers, mealy bugs, mites, moths, slugs, snails, squash bugs, striped cucumber beetles, thrips, weevils, white flies, and other sucking/chewing pests. Discourages deer, mice, rats, squirrels, and some other mammals from bothering your garden. Also reduces mildew, damping off, and other fungal infections.

Try the version without the chrysanthemum first, as it is less harmful to beneficial insects. If that doesn't clear up the pest problem, make another batch with chrysanthemum for the heavy-duty pyrethrins, but take care not to spray it on bees, butterflies, or other desirable insects.

Herbal Flea Powder

½ cup dried chrysanthemum

½ cup dried lavender flowers

¼ cup dried mint

⅛ cup dried rue

⅛ cup dried wormwood

1½ cups talcum powder

¼ cup dried pennyroyal (for dogs only)

1. Grind all of the dried herbs to a fine powder and mix them together.

2. Put the herbal powder into a large "shaker" container such as used for dispensing parsley flakes.

3. Add talcum powder. Seal the container tightly and shake to combine.

4. Sprinkle flea powder into pet's fur. For prevention or a minor flea infestation, you can brush it out after an hour. For a more serious infestation, leave it in and re-apply once a week.

Moth Balls

2 ounces paraffin wax

1 tablespoon lavender oil

1 tablespoon neem oil

½ teaspoon cedar oil

½ teaspoon mint oil

½ ounce dried chrysanthemum

½ ounce dried tansy

1. Melt the paraffin wax. Immediately pour in lavender oil, neem oil, cedar oil, and mint oil. Stir to combine.

2. Add dried chrysanthemum and dried tansy; stir again.

3. Pour the wax into small molds, or into small tins with perforated lids. Loose herbal mothballs should be kept in a dish, in case they get tacky from heat.

4. Place in drawers, chests, or closets to repel moths.

Resources

Berthold-Bond, Annie. *Better Basics for the Home: Simple Solutions for Less Toxic Living.* New York: Three Rivers Press, 1999.

Bremness, Lesley. *The Complete Book of Herbs: A Practical Guide to Growing & Using Herbs.* New York: Viking Studio Books, 1988.

Kowalchik, Claire, and William H. Hylton, editors. *Rodale's Illustrated Encyclopedia of Herbs.* New York: Rodale Press, 1987.

Herb
Crafts

Essential Crafting Tools

⫷ by Susan Pesznecker ⫸

E very herbalist needs a collection of herb-crafting tools and the knowledge of how to use them. Whether working with a sickle or a boline, a pair of garden shears or a hori-hori, a pestle or a molcajete, knowing how and when to use the right tools is part of your path to developing better practices. These tools also add to the sacred feeling you experience when working with herbs.

Workspace

Your equipment must be easy to handle and made of safe, nonreactive materials. Rely on glass, silver, and stainless steel when working with herbs, and avoid aluminum and copper. Look for well-made, high-quality tools.

The kitchen is an ideal place to work with herbs. Dedicate a drawer or cupboard for your materials, and store your herbs and oils in a cool, dark location. Light and heat are enemies of herbal potency. Your storage space should be convenient but out of the reach of babies, children, and pets.

Keep careful written records of your herbal workings. Then you'll be able to repeat your successes, and adjust as necessary when a project fizzles.

Follow sensible safety guidelines. Don't swallow something unless you know it's safe to do so. Be aware of potential interactions between herbs and medication, both prescribed and over the counter. Always use fresh ingredients, and store preparations only for the recommended time. Discard those whose time has expired.

Tools for Gathering Herbs

Of all the basic supplies you need to dig, cut, or gather herbs and roots, the most important is a cutting tool. Whatever your choice of tool, it must have a sharp blade that cuts the plant precisely and without trauma.

Basket

Choose one that is big enough to allow the cut herbs to lay flat and deep enough that they don't tumble out. Line with pieces of newspaper for absorbency and cushioning.

Boline (Bolline)

This is a white-handled blade used specifically for cutting herbs. The blade may be straight or crescent-shaped and is usually small.

Digging Stick

Many First People still use digging sticks to grub for plants and roots. These sticks are thick, fire-hardened, and typically pointed on one end. When digging, the pointed tip is inserted into the dirt around the plant and rocked back and forth to loosen the roots.

Garden Gloves

Gloves are available in cloth, leather, rubberized cloth, and blends, and will keep your hands clean and protected from thorns, insects, pests, etc. Rinse dirty gloves well and wash in warm soapy water or in a gentle washing machine cycle. Air dry. Keep two pairs of gloves so one is always ready for use.

Garden Shears

These handheld, scissor-like tools are useful for cutting stems and small branches. My favorite shears is the Felco's #7, which has a rotating grip for comfort and replaceable parts. These shears aren't cheap, but with care they'll last forever.

Hori-hori

This Japanese tool has a heavy steel cutting blade that is serrated on one side. The blade is thick enough to use as a digging tool and sharp enough for cutting, and the serrated edge saws through finger-sized branches. The wooden handle is sturdy and easy to hold.

Kneeling Pad

This thick rubber pad saves your knees and keeps your pants clean.

Loppers

These shears have long handles and are used to trim tall branches or vineing herbs.

Pruning Saw

This small, serrated saw folds into a curved wooden handle. Use a pruning saw to cut small branches and shape shrubs and trees.

Sickle

The sickle is a large, curved blade mounted on a long handle, and is used to cut large swathes of grasses. Cutting tools will last for many years if you take good care of them. After use, wash the blades and carefully dry them with a soft towel before storing with the blades closed or holstered. Wipe the blades with light machine oil about once a month, and use linseed oil on wooden parts when they look or feel dry.

Tools for Processing and Storing Herbs

Once you begin acquiring a store of herbs, you'll need tools for storage and organization.

Cellophane Bags

While these aren't good for long-term storage, they're a nice way to gift or share herbs. Buy at craft stores.

Cookie Sheets or Trays

Line cookie sheets or other large trays with newspaper. Shake the moisture from the cleaned herbs (see "sink or basin" on page 190) and lay the herbs on the sheets to dry in a warm room.

Dehydrator

In most cases, I don't recommend a dehydrator to dry herbs as the heat causes much of the volatile (essential) oils to be lost and also can change the herbs' appearance. Dehydrators works well for drying really wet substances that can mold easily, such as fruit peels. If you use a dehydrator, select low heat and dry for the briefest time possible.

Jars and Containers

Lidded jars provide ideal storage. Blue and amber are traditional colors for herbal glassware, but the glass color really doesn't matter as long as the herbs are stored in the dark. Canning (Mason) jars and clean food-grade jars with tight lids work well, too. Many herbalists don't use plastic, but a food-grade plastic jar with lid is probably as safe as glass as long as the jar isn't heated. Plastic jars and containers are ideal for freezing herbs.

Labels

Develop a labeling system for all of your herbs. Trust me: if you don't, you'll forget which is which. Many herbs look alike and smell somewhat similar when dried; so until you become familiar with them it's hard to distinguish one from another.

Microwave

I do not recommend the microwave for drying herbs as too much scent and flavor are lost in the process.

Paper Lunch Bags

Some herbs, especially those with woody stems like lavender, may be bundled and hung upside down to dry. Tie a lunch-sized paper bag loosely around the herb bundle in order to prevent dried materials from dropping and making a mess. But don't make it airtight because the herbs need circulating air in order to dry.

Salad Spinner

This is a great tool to remove excess water from fresh herbs before drying.

Sink or Basin

Immerse freshly harvested herbs in a tub of clean, cold water and add one to two tablespoons of salt or vinegar to the water to help remove dirt and insects. Soak for twenty to thirty minutes, swishing the herbs with your hands now and then. Rinse the herbs with fresh water and shake dry on cotton towels. Or use a salad spinner.

Steel Tins

These are good for loose, dried herbs and also for storing tea bags and holding balms and waxes. They aren't completely airtight so they should not be used for long-term storage.

String

Fresh herbs with woody stems such as lavender and rosemary can be bundled loosely and hung upside down to dry. However, be sure there is no surface moisture on the herbs before hanging. Use natural fiber string such as cotton, jute, or hemp.

Zipper Bags

These plastic bags are useful when gathering herbs, especially small items like berries and rose hips. They're also great for freezing herbs and for storing dried materials.

Tools for Preparing Herbs

Most people do the bulk of their herbal work in the kitchen. You may be lucky enough to have a separate set of materials dedicated to your herbal workings, but there's no reason you can't use some or all of your usual kitchenware. Or you might rely mostly on your usual kitchen supplies but keep a few special pieces, such as a separate set of measuring spoons, to be used only with your herbs.

Cutting Boards

Some people believe that plastic or glass cutting boards are more sanitary, but recent studies show that wood boards can be kept equally clean. Choose the size and kind of cutting board that best fits your purposes.

Double Boiler

Use a double boiler to heat or melt flammable materials such as paraffin, or any substance, such as chocolate, which can be ruined by direct heat.

Funnels

These are used when pouring solutions between containers.

Garlic Press

This is used to extract garlic pulp and juice from a peeled garlic clove.

Graters

Regular-bore graters are useful for shaving and breaking down stiff materials like hard cocoa butter. A microplane grater is ideal for grating hard materials like whole nutmegs, and it also does a beautiful job of fine-grating citrus peels.

Grinders

A coffee bean grinder can be used to grind dry herbs and spices.

Grinding Stone

Search for a heavy, flat stone with a central depression to use as a mortar, and find a second stone as the pestle. Mexican cooks use a grinding stone made of volcanic stone called a *metate* (may-TAH-tay).

Infuser

Fresh or dried herbs and spices can be put into an infuser, which is immersed in liquid, allowing the herbs within to infuse into the liquid. Infusers are shaped as balls, wands, spoons, or cup inserts. Most are metal, but some, especially cup inserts, are made of mesh plastic. It's also possible to buy infusing teapots with a built-in removable infuser.

Knives and Cleavers

A set of sharp knives and a small cleaver are useful for chopping herbs. The mezzaluna ("half-moon") is a single or double curved blade designed for chopping herbs. It has a handle on each end.

Laboratory Glass

If you have a bit of mad scientist lurking within, visit science supply stores for flasks, beakers, and laboratory ware. These items are heat-proof and made of glass, Plexiglas, or inert plastic.

Measuring Tools

Keep two sets of measuring cups, one for liquids and one for solids, and a set of good measuring spoons.

Mortar and Pestle

This is a traditional tool for grinding spices and hard herbal parts such as bark and dried berries. A non-metallic mortar and pestle is best, and many are made from marble or soapstone. The molcajete (mohl-cah-HAY-tay) is a Mexican mortar made from volcanic rock.

Peelers and Zesters

These are useful to produce citrus zest, peel ginger, or remove bark from twigs.

Saucepans

You will need various sizes of saucepans in glass or stainless steel. Avoid aluminum, iron, and copper as these react with many herbs, changing their color, scent, taste, or essential nature.

Scales

A food-grade scale is invaluable for accurately weighing materials.

Spoons

Large spoons made of wood, steel, or silver are helpful to stir mixtures. Small silver spoons are traditional for tea.

Strainers

These come in wire, metal, and plastic in different mesh sizes. The smaller the holes, the clearer the liquid will be. On the other hand, if you drink an infusion without straining it, you can always read the tea leaves afterwards. Cheesecloth is also an effective strainer; use two or more layers.

Teacups and Mugs

These are useful for making culinary or medicinal infusions, and clear mugs are helpful in assessing the brew's color and clarity. If you want to try tasseomancy (tealeaf reading), invest in plain white teacups with saucers.

Teapots and Kettles

Tea kettles are usually metal, and teapots are usually made of glass or ceramic. Some Asian-style pots are made of cast iron, which holds heat for a long time.

Herbal Ingredients

Alcohol

Use grain alcohol (ethanol)—never wood alcohol (isopropyl or rubbing alcohol). A 190-proof grain alcohol is ideal, and you can also use high-quality vodka (140 proof). If you use wine in recipes, buy the best you can afford.

Carrier Oils

These inert, plant-based oils (sunflower, apricot, grapeseed, etc.) are used as a base in a recipe or working. Most carrier oils have little or no aroma and a neutral color and consistency. Store in the refrigerator for longest life.

Clays

These are mineral substances retrieved from soil deposits. Kaolin is an astringent (drying) clay used topically for facials and other skin treatments.

Essential (volatile) Oil

This is a natural oil typically obtained by distillation and having the characteristic fragrance of the plant or other source from which it is extracted. Each is a highly concentrated essence with strong scent and flavor.

Jellies and Ointments

Petroleum jelly is an oil-based product used in some balms and salves. It has a vaguely metallic smell and can be melted. Zinc-oxide ointment—a heavy, white cream that includes mineral oil and petroleum jelly—is used to protect the skin from sun exposure.

Mineral Oil

This is a petroleum product not generally used by herbologists.

Sugars and Syrups

Use unrefined or raw sugar, honey, pure maple syrup, or dark molasses. These natural sugars yield the purest (and tastiest!) results in your herbal workings.

Salts

Work with sea salt or non-iodized salt, which are free of artificial ingredients. Epsom salts (magnesium chloride) are often added to baths and foot soaks.

Tincture of Benzoin

This substance is added to balms and ointments as a preservative. Purchase at the local pharmacy.

Vinegars

Use white vinegar or follow your recipe. Choose organic vinegars when possible.

Water

Good water is critical in herbal recipes, so consider using bottled spring water, especially if your home water supply is questionable.

Note: Rainwater isn't a safe substitute as it is often contaminated with pollutants.

Waxes and Fats

These are plant- and animal-based substances used to prepare balms and creams. Cocoa butter comes from cacao beans, and unrefined cocoa butter is yellowish, firm, and smells like chocolate. (A balm made from cocoa butter and peppermint oil smells like a peppermint patty!) Beeswax is taken from honeycomb and is soft, malleable, and smells of honey. Refined vegetable shortening and animal tallow can also be used for a preparation known as enfleurage, where herbal essences are infused into solid fats. Paraffin is a petroleum-based wax used to prepare candles and some ointments.

Witch Hazel

This clear, astringent liquid made from the witch hazel plant is used in skin-care preparations, and it soothes sunburn.

Herbal Miscellany

Many of these tools and materials are used in daily herbal practices.

Censer

This container in which incense is burned is made from metal and has perforations to allow smoke to escape.

Charcoal

These rounds of compressed charcoal are used for burning loose herbal incense. Place them in a thurible or on a fireproof surface, pile herbs on the charcoal, and light.

Cheesecloth

This gauzy, cotton fabric used in cooking gets it name from its use in wrapping unripe cheeses during the curing process. It can be used as a strainer, as a giant teabag in a bathtub or foot soak, or to bind a poultice.

Fillable Teabags

These paper teabags can be filled as desired and closed by ironing or self-adhesion. Bath teabags are big enough to infuse a tub of bath water.

Muslin

This unbleached cotton fabric is used to make herb or bath bags, sachets, charms, etc. It's also an excellent binder for poultices and plasters.

Thurible

A thurible is any open container used to burn herbs or loose incense. An abalone shell is often used for a thurible.

Vial (phial)

This is a small glass or plastic container closed by a stopper or screw-top lid or a dropper, spray, or roller end.

The Well-Read Herbalist

Building a good reference library is another important tool. Although there is a vast amount of information on the Internet, it's not the same as curling up in a chair with a cup of tea and a favorite book, or propping a book open on the counter while trying a new herbal infusion.

Ask your teachers and herbal mentors for book suggestions, and search bookstores, libraries, and online booksellers. Most books also include a recommended reading or resource list.

Sunflowers

⤳ by JD Hortwort ⤳

The sunflower (*Helianthus annuus*) is a universal sign of summer. This beauty comes in many varieties, including the well-known giant Mammoth sunflower that can grow to fifteen feet tall and is perhaps the one that comes to mind most readily. But gardeners can find varieties that grow to as few as three feet. Some sunflowers produce single flowers on single stalks and others have multiple flowers. There are even perennial sunflowers.

Sunflowers grow quickly and easily in well-amended soil in a sunny location. They thrive in the heat of summer, if provided with plenty of water. Then, before you know it, late summer arrives and it's time

to harvest. While sunflowers will dry very well on the stalk, you may find yourself fighting the birds and squirrels for your sunflower treats. Also, if you are growing the giant varieties to make crafts, you may find that natural drying results in a curled flower head that is hard to work with.

Harvesting Sunflowers

Unlike some flowers traditionally used for drying, sunflower petals don't hold to the flower head very well as they dry. You can gather the petals for use in potpourri but don't expect a harvested sunflower of any size to hang onto its petals.

If you grow small varieties, cut the stem to a length of at least twelve inches when you see the petals start to fade. These stems can then be bundled together and dried by hanging them upside down in any cool, dark, dry location. Later, you can use the seed heads in dried flower arrangements, or gather the seeds for bird feed.

If you grow giant sunflowers, watch for the back of the blossom to begin to yellow, which means it's safe to harvest the flower. Cut the stem about twelve inches long, carefully run a piece of floral wire through the thickest part of the stem, and hang the flower upside down to dry. This technique, however, could still allow the flower head to curl.

If you need a nice, flat seed head, cut small holes in a mesh screen and set the flower right side up, with the stem threaded through the holes. Set the screen on sawhorses in the shed or in a warm, dry area out of the sun. The length of the drying process will vary according to the weather.

Once your treasures are dry, if you want to use them later, wrap the dried seed heads in several layers of newspaper and store in a plastic container away from light and humidity.

Using Sunflowers

Treats for Birds

Birds love sunflower heads, and it's easy to create this tasty treat for them. Bore a hole in the seed head about two inches from the edge, run a wire through the hole, and hang the flower head from a tree branch close to the house so you can watch them. Two flower heads can be wired together, back to back, doubling the pleasure for your feathery friends.

Don't worry if the flower heads have curled despite your best efforts. Pack the back of the flower head with suet, string a wire through the flower head, and hang in a tree. You can purchase suet from most garden stores or make your own. The Internet is a great source for suet recipes, and many can be mixed to attract specific types of birds.

Suet is rendered beef fat, and the easiest recipe is to melt together equal amounts of suet and peanut butter. (You can use lard instead of suet.) Then stir bird seed into the mix, using as much seed as the mixture will hold. Pack the end result onto the back of the flower head and allow it to cool and set. Then hang the treat from a tree and get ready to watch the fun.

If you don't have any full sunflower heads to use as a suet holder, you can pack your suet around a sturdy twine. Shape it into a ball or into a long, slender tube like a sausage. Then roll the suet in sunflower seeds and allow it to set. You can make many of these and freeze them for later use.

Decorative Sunflower Wreath

You can also create a decorative sunflower with a seed head, a straw wreath, and some dried apple slices. Cut the dried apple slices in half to mimic the long narrow shape of the flower petals. If you don't want to cut the slices, you can overlap them so that only one-third to one-half of each slice is showing. Using floral pins, attach the slices to the wreath. For a really full looking sunflower, you can create two or more layers of dried apple slices.

Then bore four holes in a flat seed head—north, south, east, and west, and using light-gauge wire, tie the seed head to the center of the straw wreath. You can hide the wire by carefully sliding it under the apple slices.

A word of caution: If you hang this project on the outside door, expect all the birds and squirrels in the neighborhood to be knocking on your door until the seeds are gone!

Aromatherapy

⟡ by Calantirniel ⟡

A romatherapy is the art and science of using the natural properties of plants, called essential oils, to help heal physical, emotional, mental, and even spiritual dis-ease. Today, it continues to experience a revival because people are rediscovering and allowing authentic, very "alive" scents to (re)educate their bodies, minds, and souls—and, therefore, healing on all levels. The practice of aromatherapy can take years to master.

Essential oils are created through distillation, a practice that has been in use for thousands of years. But it lost popularity when clever marketing of cheaper synthetic chemicals became available (and this can still be a problem, so investigate before purchase). Man-made, life-less chemicals do not have the same healing effects and can sometimes have the opposite effect. Steam is the most common distilling method. Another method, solvent extraction, preserves essential oils for a very long time.

The extremely concentrated nature of essential oils and the fact that they can (through smell) quickly pass the blood-brain barrier, are reasons to be careful when using them. However, there are guidelines that you can immediately implement to great benefit if you are a beginner.

The First Step

Begin your journey with the most versatile essential oil: lavender (*Lavandula spp.*, which means "to wash" in Latin). The bluish-purple flowers tell us it aligns with the crown and third-eye chakras and is a healing color for all chakras. This helps to account for the versatility of this wonderful first choice. Lavender smells clean, fresh, and not too flowery; it is a calming mood elevator that relaxes nerves and relieves stress. It also stimulates focus and concentration, and if needed, provides energy to accomplish a task.

The hybrid lavender, called *Lavandin*, has more menthol (also found in mint, camphor, and eucalyptus essential oils). Although it smells different, it can still provide healing as long as it is a pure, steam-distilled essential oil.

Store lavender essential oil in a glass container (colored is best) that has a hard plastic cap, and keep in a cool, dark place. Use a glass dropper to dispense. Essential oils are so strong that they often melt plastic, thereby bringing the chemicals of the plastic into the bottle's contents (not to mention the leaky mess).

Lavender's healing properties are analgesic, antibiotic, anti-convulsive, antidepressant, antiseptic, antispasmodic, antiviral, antitoxic, cicatrisant, decongestant, sedative, and stimulant. It can be used as a study aid, to overcome emotions, to decrease stress, to treat headaches, to help heal burns and wounds with minimal scarring, and to improve hair and scalp health (even head lice). Lavender can be used for nearly anything that needs to be cleansed or purified. If you treat animals, especially cats, with lavender, first do extensive research and then use caution. There may be better herbal alternatives for animals.

Ways to Use Essential Oils

Bath Salts

Thoroughly mix together ⅓ cup table or sea salt, one-third cup baking soda, and ⅓ cup Epsom salts. Add between 10 and 30 drops of essential oil, depending on strength of the smell, and thoroughly mix by mashing with your hands. Add to bath (add more Epsom salts if you wish) and de-stress! This can also be used as a skin scrub (go easy, especially around your face), and even to clean surfaces like counters, sinks, bathtubs. Add enough water to make a paste, then wipe down surfaces. Store unused amounts in a moisture-proof jar, away from heat.

Cologne and Room Sprays

Use a glass bottle with a quality spray device. A good proportion is approximately 7 to 12 drops essential oil to 4 ounces distilled water. Before adding the water, place a teaspoon of vodka or brandy in the mix to preserve it.

Massage and Hair/Scalp Treatment

Use a cold-pressed base oil such as olive oil (better for dry skin) or grapeseed oil (better for oily skin), with a mixing ratio of 2 to 5 drops essential oil per teaspoon of base oil. Warm the oil in your hands before applying. For head lice, rinse hair with vinegar, then shower, and do an initial scalp treatment the first day in conjunction with a twice a day use of a Lice-meister comb for 14 days. Make sure the comb is completely clean between uses. If it is not, you will need to restart the count and the program.

Neat

This essential oil is undiluted, and the only ones you can use this way, without research, are lavender and tea tree. Any others may damage your skin. Try using these two oils neat for itches, wounds, and burns; both minimize or eliminate scarring. Apply lavender on temples for improved studying or headache relief. Some oils can promote wellness when placed on a pillow and inhaled (oils do cause stains, so take necessary precautions to protect your linens).

The Next Step

After experiencing the healing powers of lavender, you may want to expand your collection of essential oils. All essential oils work immediately and are finished with their healing work within a few minutes. Then the body catches up. It can be very confusing to know which ones to choose because there are so many and so many healing qualities. However, often it is the smell that can help you determine what to get next.

If the intention is to combine essential oils into a new smell (called a blend), try the following method: Open two essential oil bottles, hold them together and smell while running your nose above both bottles. If an essential oil or the combination doesn't smell good, smell fresh coffee beans to cancel the effect and start over. If one is too strong, move that bottle lower below your nose and smell again.

When you have selected your oils, place one drop of the stronger one and as many drops as you need of the weaker one to achieve the desired smell into a new glass bottle. Close both of the essential oils and store. If you want to add another essential oil to the blend, open it next to the current work-in-progress and, again, drop it back if too strong. Soon you will know exactly which essential oils to use and how much. Once completed, add your base oil or use the essential oil mixture in bath salts or a room spray. Name your blend, and add it to your aromatherapy recipe journal. Then you won't have to repeat this process every time!

Note: If you are pregnant, check the use of an essential oil with a knowledgeable practitioner. If you are on high-potency homeopathic remedies, you may wish to avoid menthol, camphor, and essential oils with tea tree, eucalyptus, and peppermint. They may inadvertently cancel your remedy.

The system below has four groupings (and one subgroup) that may help simplify the process of choosing the right essential oils to assist you and your family's particular healing needs. Nearly all essential oils are on some level antibacterial, antiviral, or antimicrobial, and some are even antiparasital or antifungal. After doing research on each one, let your nose guide you! Try one from each category, and gradually build your aromatherapy collection gradually.

Purification (Cooling)

In this group, are the most useful essential oils, and these will likely end up being more than half of your collection. This group of essential oils has a clean and sometimes medicinal smell, tends to break up stagnant energy and stimulate, and will counter inflammation, kill infection, or eliminate toxins, providing a clean foundation for the next stage of healing (which is often physical at this level). Good for oily skin.

Basil

Basil stimulants the conscious mind and is useful for mental fatigue (good to smell while driving long distances), insect bites/repellent, gout, cramps, diarrhea (with chamomile), happiness, peace, prosperity, love, and decisions.

Cypress

Useful for overcoming loss and easing transitions, bed-wetting, female issues, asthma, hemorrhoids, colds, and invigorating muscles.

Eucalyptus

Aids breathing and lungs, muscle pain, cold sores, healing, and purification of negativity, and is a decongestant.

Hyssop

Useful for purification (spiritual and mental), the conscious mind, colds, coughs, hypertension, and dermatitis, it clears the head and dispels bad vibrations.

Juniper

Useful for kidney, bladder, and urinary issues, detoxification, and muscle pain—especially when used with ylang-ylang.

Peppermint

Aids purification, conscious mind, headache, indigestion, acne, dermatitis, chicken pox, ringworm, aches, palpitations. Relieves gas, lung issues, decongestant. Good for dream work, but if peppermint is too intense, try spearmint.

Pine

Promotes purification, healing, protection, prosperity, and physical energy (inhale during recuperation), is good for sinusitis, muscle aches, sprains, house cleaning, and repels negativity. If pine is too strong, try lighter evergreens like spruce or fir.

Rosemary

Promotes longevity, the conscious mind, memory, stimulating, promotes and secures love, antiseptic, acne, dermatitis, scalp treatment, and hair regrowth.

Tea Tree

Tea tree is antiparasital, antifungal, and antiseptic, and good for wounds (prevents scarring), colds, gums (numbs pain), acne, athlete's foot, candida, muscle pain, cold sores, sunburn, ticks, head lice, and as a decongestant household cleaner.

Thyme (White)

Useful for throat infections (cough, laryngitis), gums, insect bites, circulation, eczema, and bronchitis.

Purification (Warming)

This subgroup also purifies, but uses warming, spicy stimulating essential oils rather than the cooling action of the essential oils listed above. Always dilute these.

Black Pepper

Benefits physical energy and mental alertness (try when driving), eases pain and constipation, builds courage, repels negativity, and is protective.

Cinnamon

This is often called cassia. Do not use on skin. Raises physical energy and awareness; attracts love and wealth.

Cardamom

It is similar to fennel, without the licorice smell, and can be used to attract love.

Clove

This oil has a very strong smell and is used for teeth pain, muscle pain, and circulation. It eliminates garlic odor.

Cumin

It has a strong odor and is used to repel or banish unwanted energies, and for protection and healing.

Fennel

This has a licorice smell, reduces spasm, relieves flatulence, and is good for digestion and cellulite.

Ginger

Improves circulation, especially in the lower body and extremities. Relieves muscle pain, flatulence, coughs, chills, and debility; acts as a decongestant; builds energy, physical love, and prosperity.

Nutmeg

Less intense than clove. Good for muscle pain, the kidneys and uterus; digestion, frigidity, and psychic development. It is a psychic energy builder and a powerful builder for prosperity.

Citrus

These essential oils are usually cold-pressed rather than steam-distilled and are photosensitive, so don't apply before going in the sun. This group also has a clean smell, without smelling medicinal. Instead, these oils are fresh and light, sometimes sweet. They enhance feelings of happiness and uplift the mood and mental state. These essential oils help oily or acne-prone skin.

Bergamot

A natural flavoring in Earl Grey tea, it is used to treat cold sores and mouth infections, acne, insect bites, and depression. It also enhances peace, happiness, and restful sleep.

Citronella

Similar to lemon grass, this is most often used as an insect repellent, particularly for mosquitoes.

Grapefruit

This is the best citrus for water retention and lymphatic stimulation.

Lemon and Lime

These can be used interchangeably for purification, health, healing, physical energy, food poisoning, hair/skin care (lightens hair, especially when combined with chamomile), insect bites, and mouth/skin ulcers. Astringents, they are invigorating and stimulating.

Lemon Grass

Use this for purification, insect repellent, oily/acne skin, and psychic awareness. It adds shine to hair and attracts bees.

Orange

Promotes joy, purification, physical energy, magical energy, an uplifting mood, good cheer, and sleep. It is refreshing and counteracts water retention, intestinal problems, constipation, colds, nervous stress, bronchitis, and dull, oily skin. Tangerine has similar qualities and is sometimes preferred. Sweet orange is somewhere between orange and neroli, is used for love, and combats depression.

Sweet

This group could easily be named "florals," but not all of them are made with the flowering part of the plants. These essential oils are most effective on the emotional level, allowing love into our hearts, calming our nerves, relieving worry, providing stability, and bringing about thoughts and feelings of security and well-being. Physically, many are good for dry or mature skin. Some, like rose, jasmine, and neroli, are very expensive if authentic.

Chamomile

This oil is good for relaxation, calming nerves, sleep, digestion, colic, gas, and diarrhea (with basil), and for lightening hair (especially with lemon).

Calendula

A calming oil, it is useful for all skin problems, including acne, burns, eczema, insect bites, and wounds. It promotes health, sleep, and psychic dreams.

Carrot

An antioxidant, it increases elasticity in mature skin, and is good for acne, liver congestion, and prosperity.

Geranium

This is uplifting and promotes happiness, and is useful as a sedative and for nervousness, acne, eczema, sore throat, female complaints, and head lice. It is an excellent substitute for the more expensive rose (especially rose geranium).

Jasmine

This oil promotes love, peace, spirituality, sex, sleep, and psychic or prophetic dreams, and is useful for uterine and female complaints, dry skin, depression, nervousness, and worry.

Neroli

Also called orange blossom, this oil promotes deep joy, purification, love, and sex, and is useful for anxiety, stretch marks, and depression. It is an emotional stabilizer.

Palmarosa

This smell is between rose and lemon grass and it attracts love, and speeds healing with complementary treatments. It is good for acne, dermatitis, scars, wrinkles, intestinal infections and stress, and moisturizes the skin.

Rose

This is good for love, peace, beauty, sex, anxiety, depression, circulation, broken capillaries, conjunctivitis, dry skin, skin ulcers, irregular menstruation, frigidity, headache, and appearance, and it opens the heart chakra.

Vanilla

This is useful for physical energy, attraction, love, sex, magical energy, and as an antidepressant. It is arousing, especially for men.

Ylang-Ylang

The "flower of flowers," it enhances peace, sex, and love, relaxes nerves, arouses and heightens pleasure, and promotes physical energy. It combines well with juniper for a muscle-ache massage.

Earthy

These essential oils are often resinous, and smell woodsy, mossy, or even like soil. While some are elevating and some are heavy, all are grounding and work on the physical plane. A few work well on the spiritual plane. They restore strength and energy, and provide a feeling of centeredness and even protection, and are good for oily and acne-prone skin and dry, mature skin.

Cedarwood

An antifungal, this oil promotes spirituality, meditation, and self-control, and is good for coughs, colds, flu, and greasy hair/oily skin, and repels insects.

Clary Sage

Good for female complaints (uterine/menstrual, frigidity), it combines well with other essential oils (try geranium and sweet orange), and is relaxant and that promotes euphoria, calm, and dreams. It is useful for high blood pressure, asthma, throat infection, colic, and depression.

Frankincense

Use this oil for spirituality, peace, meditation, mystical power, wounds, and mature skin, and as an incense base.

Myrrh

This oil is useful for spirituality, meditation, healing, love, awareness, cold sores (with patchouli), gum infections, voice loss, and arthritis, and for rejuvenating skin (wrinkles) and calming worry.

Patchouli

A mood enhancer, this oil promotes physical energy, re-laxation, money, and protection, and is useful for frigidity, nervous exhaustion, sex, acne, sores (for cold sores, combine with myrrh), athlete's foot, and dry or oily skin.

Rosewood

This calms nerves, builds the immune system, removes musty smells, and is useful for frigidity, acne, scars, dermatitis, scalp, colds, coughs, and fever.

Sandalwood

This oil is useful for spirituality, healing, meditation, sex/aphrodisiac, urinary infections, respiratory, throat issues (including strep), and is used for all offerings to any deity (always accepted).

ଐ ଐ ଐ

Enjoy your aromatherapy journey, and may you find happiness and healing in all you experience!

Resources

Cunningham, Scott. *Magical Aromatherapy*. St. Paul, MN: Llewellyn Publications, 1989.

Grace, Kendra. *Aromatherapy Pocketbook* (2nd ed.). Woodbury, MN: Llewellyn Worldwide Ltd., 1999.

Rose, Jeanne. *The Aromatherapy Book*. Berkeley, CA: North Atlantic Books, 1992.

Various Essential Oils Pocket Reference (3rd ed.). Orem, UT: Essential Science Publishing, 2005.

Worwood, Valerie Ann. *The Complete Book of Essential Oils and Aromatherapy*. San Rafael, CA: New World Library, 1991.

Fragrant Graces

≈ by Elizabeth Barrette ≈

C ertain herbs that have an especially strong scent are grown for fragrance and craft materials, and they can also be purchased in dried form or as essential oils. Crafts made with fragrant herbs awaken your senses and make your home smell good.

Aromatherapy Scents

Herbs with strong scents are the basis of aromatherapy, a practice that uses the active components of plants to influence moods and provide other benefits. By blending the leaves, flowers, woody parts, and/or essential oils of these plants we can harness their properties.

If you grow your own herbs, you know they're real and whether they were organically grown. When shopping, however, you need to be careful. Chemicals from pesticides or other sources can contaminate cheaply produced herbal materials. There are also artificial "fragrance" oils that have nothing to do with the real plants and thus don't have the same mystical or therapeutic qualities. Buy organic herbs and real essential oils if at all possible. However, some scents are not available as essential oils.

For best results, each craft project should include a variety of herbs, with scents from what are called top (or high), middle (or heart), and base (or low) notes. Top notes are sharp; they're noticed first but fade quickly. Middle notes are more mellow and complex. Base notes can be subtle, bitter, or unusual, but they bind the other notes and help them last. Some herbs spread their fragrance across two levels, making them excellent for connecting others. Following are some common herbs and their notes:

> **Top:** Bergamot (to middle), camphor, cinnamon, Clary sage (to middle), coriander (to middle), eucalyptus, galangal (to middle), grapefruit, hyssop (to middle), lavender (to middle), lemon, lime, neroli (to middle), orange, peppermint, sage, sweet basil (to middle), sweetgrass (to middle), tea tree (to middle), thyme (to middle)

> **Middle:** Cardamom, chamomile, cypress, gardenia, geranium, ginger (to base) juniper, oregano, orris root, mugwort, sweet marjoram, pine, rosemary, ylang-ylang (to base)

Base: Benzoin, cedar, copal, frankincense, galbanum, hops, jasmine, myrrh, patchouli, rose, sandalwood, vanilla

Aromatherapy is also based on its effects, and each herb can have a variety of properties. When you combine herbs with the same or complementary properties, the effect is strengthened. Following are some events and their associated herbs:

Purification: Benzoin, camphor, cedar, copal, cypress, eucalyptus, frankincense, hyssop, lavender, lemon, myrrh, orange, oregano, peppermint, pine, rosemary, sandalwood, tea tree, thyme

Romantic: Cardamom, cedar, cinnamon, frankincense, galangal, galbanum, gardenia, ginger, jasmine, lime, myrrh, orange, patchouli, pine, rose, rosemary, sandalwood, sweet basil, vanilla, ylang-ylang

Soothing: Bergamot, chamomile, Clary sage, cypress, ginger, hops, jasmine, lavender, lemon, mugwort, rose, sweet marjoram, vanilla

Uplifting: Eucalyptus, geranium, grapefruit, juniper, lavender, lemon, lime, orange, peppermint, pine, rosemary, sweet basil, tea tree, ylang-ylang

Fragrant Craft Projects

Many traditional craft projects make use of fragrant herbs, and each of the following recipes matches one of the moods previously mentioned. However, you can also use these recipes as inspiration for creating your own with different scents.

For example, you might want a soothing incense for meditation or a romantic fabric softener for the bedroom. Just be sure to use natural ingredients, and include a balance of top, middle, and bottom notes.

Powerful Purification Potpourri

3 cups dried peppermint leaves

10 drops lavender oil

2 cups dried lavender buds

10 drops pine oil

1 cup miniature pine cones

½ cup cedar chips

½ cup sandalwood chips

½ cup orris root chips

1. Place 3 cups dried peppermint leaves in a large, opaque, resealable container. Add lavender oil to dried lavender buds, toss gently to combine, and let the oil soak in. Add pine oil to miniature pine cones, toss gently to combine, and let it soak.

2. Pour the lavender buds and the pine cones into the peppermint leaves and stir to combine. Add cedar chips, sandalwood chips, and orris root chips.

3. Seal the container tightly and shake well.

4. Store in a warm, dry place for one month, shaking the container daily to distribute and blend the scents.

5. Place the potpourri in smaller sealed containers and open one when you want to scent the room. Alternatively, you can put a small amount into a lidded basket

for constant fragrance, but you'll need to replace the potpourri more often or add fresh oils.

Soothing Floral Fabric Softener

2 cups baking soda

2 cups white vinegar

1 quart water

¼ ounce lavender oil

⅛ ounce rose oil

⅛ ounce vanilla oil

⅛ ounce neroli oil

1. In a large plastic or glass container, combine baking soda and white vinegar. The mixture should fizz, so wait for it to settle down before stirring in water. Add lavender oil, rose oil, and vanilla oil, stir again, and seal the container.

2. Add ¼ cup to your washing machine during the rinse cycle. But don't combine this with bleach, as the vinegar can create stinky fumes.

Alternatively, you can make dryer sheets by layering strips of flannel in a resealable container. Pour the fabric softener over the flannel, covering them, seal the container, and let rest for two days. Take one strip, squeeze out the excess liquid, and place the damp strip in your dryer with the laundry. Keep the container sealed.

Spicy Romantic Firestarters

2 pounds paraffin or beeswax

3 cups pine sawdust

2 cups cedar wood chips

½ cup dried sweet basil

½ cup dried rosemary

⅓ cup cinnamon bark chips

⅓ cup galangal chips

⅓ cup sandalwood chips

1. Place the wax in a double boiler or wax melter to melt.
2. Meanwhile, combine pine sawdust, cedar wood chips, dried sweet basil, dried rosemary, cinnamon bark chips, galangal chips, and sandalwood chips in a large bowl. Stir with an old wooden spoon.
3. When the wax is fully melted, pour it over the herb mixture. Stir carefully to blend, making sure that all the herb and wood pieces are completely coated with wax.
4. While the wax mixture is still warm (but not hot), press blobs of it into the cups of cardboard egg cartons.
5. Once hard, the cartons of firestarters will stack neatly. Tear off one when you're ready to start a fire, carefully pile kindling around it, and then light the cardboard edges and enjoy the fragrance. Add logs after the kindling is burning.

Uplifting Citrus Air Freshener

¾ cup water

2 packets unflavored gelatin

¼ cup unflavored vodka

20 drops lemon oil

10 drops orange oil

10 drops grapefruit oil

5 drops rosemary oil

5 drops ylang-ylang oil

1. Bring water to boil. Stir in unflavored gelatin, and cool to room temperature.
2. Add vodka. Stir in lemon oil, orange oil, grapefruit oil, rosemary oil, and ylang-ylang oil.
3. Pour the gel into a glass jar and place it in the refrigerator until set. Place a jar in a room to freshen the air.

This is a good way to reuse glass jars. Trace a pattern on a jar lid and hammer nail holes through it to make a decorative lid that allows air to circulate and carry the scent. Otherwise, leave the lid whole and remove it when in use.

Resources

Bremness, Lesley. *Herbs: The Visual Guide to More than 700 Plant Species from Around the World.* New York: DK Publishing, 1994.

Coleman, Dean. "Essential Oil Notes & Characteristics." Dean Coleman Herbal Luxuries. http://tinyurl.com/obyrzu. Accessed June 8, 2010.

Cunningham, Scott. *Cunningham's Encyclopedia of Magical Herbs*. Woodbury, MN: Llewellyn Publications, 1991.

Davis, Patricia. *Aromatherapy: An A-Z: The Most Comprehensive Guide to Aromatherapy Ever Published*. London, UK: Random House, 2005.

Hawkins, Jessie. *Herbal Crafts: More Than 60 Simple Projects to Beautify Your Home and Body*. Sandy, UT: Silverleaf Press, 2008.

Autumn Luck Bag

≫ by Lucy Hall Kelly ≪

It was the feeling that things too often go wrong in my life that motivated me to attempt to shift my luck in a positive direction. I had been struggling with money issues and trouble in relationships. I even had the silliest concern about dropping or breaking things. It seemed that just when I felt that I was over an incident and on top of my game, once again something else would happen. Reflecting on my ill luck, I had become depressed. However, during the arrival of my favorite season of the year, autumn, I became inspired.

The autumn season lasts from the Autumnal Equinox until the Winter Solstice, arriving in September and ending in December. It is an enchanting time during which night arrives earlier and the crisp scent of earth fills the air. Brilliant colors of red, brown, orange, green, and gold surround the environment with autumn foliage and harvest crops.

Autumn is not only the season that denotes the transition from summer to winter but also a transformation period and the ending of cycles. This transformation period can hold magical properties during which a transition of inviting good luck and banishing bad luck can be achieved. Fruit and nuts are harvested at this time of year, and in a magical sense one can bear mystical fruits and gain rewards for efforts, making a positive transformation and ending a cycle of ill luck. In times long past, autumn was often associated with mortality and melancholy, and in modern times, the arrival of winter can be a little depressing. However, an autumn luck bag can lift your spirits in the cold winter days to come.

Your luck bag will include items associated with generating good luck, and the bag's contents are chosen based on the number five, which is considered a lucky number. In Chinese myth, five is considered lucky because of the five elements of health, wealth, luck, life, and peace. Five is also recorded as a magical number because of the five-pointed star of protection and balance often used in the magical community.

Two herbs to use in your luck bag are basil and bay leaves. Basil, which can change luck, it is used for purification, protection, love, prosperity, and money. Bay leaves are included for protection, clairvoyance, luck, purification, and healing, and to ward off negativity that can sway luck.

There are five luck items to include in your bag. Begin with three keys bound together, which are symbolic of unlocking doors to new opportunity, wealth, and love. The acorn, nut of the oak tree, is considered a gift of youth, wealth, and attraction to anyone who chooses to carry one close. Feathers are ancient charms for luck representing a journey of the soul to other realms. The buckeye nut has been revered as a good luck charm that will increase the money in your pocket and also aid health aliments such as headaches, rheumatism, and arthritis. Add a penny to symbolize good fortune in money matters.

You can purchase a drawstring bag or make your own in autumn colors that promote personal growth and luck. Choose a bag with any of these colors:

- Orange—promotes creativity, vitality, endurance, changes, and self-esteem.
- Gold—promotes personal power, courage, confidence, will power, and success.
- Green—promotes prosperity, fertility, success, good luck, and money.
- Brown—symbolizes the earth element, stability, and reliability.
- Red—represents energy and excitement, and encourages action taken in order to achieve life goals.

If you purchase a bag with a removable drawstring, you can replace it with gold string or cord. Also have cinnamon incense on hand as it is used in ritual to promote wealth and success.

Materials Needed: Luck Charms

- Three keys
- 1 acorn
- 1 feather

- 1 buckeye

- 1 penny

You may substitute one luck charm with a lucky stone. The following contain the fall colors.

- Calcite

- Agate

- Amber

- Bloodstone

- Jasper (poppy jasper)

Other Materials

- 5 pinches of dried basil

- 5 bay leaves

- Cinnamon incense

- Green candle

- Piece of paper or parchment

- Green pen or marker

- Pouch/bag
- Gold string/cord

1. Gather your five luck objects (the three keys count one object).
2. Bind the three keys by inserting the gold string through the holes.
2. Visualize positive wants/needs/wishes. Imagine positive energy flowing into the items as you hold them in your hands, close to your heart.

3. Ask a spirit guide of choice for a blessing. Place the luck charms in the bag.
4. Using a smaller piece of paper or parchment, write the following affirmation in green ink using either a pen or marker along with personal information about yourself such as your date of birth or name.

Affirmation

May good luck be my friend in whatever I do,
May trouble always be a stranger to me,
May my pockets be heavy and my heart light,
May good luck pursue me each morning and night.

~ Irish Blessing

5. Roll up the paper, seal with a drop of wax from the candle, and place the scroll in the bag.
6. Place five pinches of herbs from the list into the bag.
7. Shake the bag to mix contents while reciting the written affirmation.
8. Do a positive activity for no particular amount of time each day for the following week while holding the finished bag.

Now that you have created your good luck bag, hold it close to your heart (heart's desire) while reciting your affirmation and visualizing positive energy soothing you and your wishes coming true. Repeat if you feel your luck is diminishing.

Herb
History,
Myth, and
Lore

Nastrutium: Sparks in the Garden

❧ by Linda Raedisch ❧

Early on in J. R. R. Tolkien's *The Fellowship of the Ring*, the wizard Gandalf delivers a cartload of fireworks to the hobbit Bilbo's residence of Bag End. Outside the parlor to which wizard and hobbit shortly repair, grow a profusion of "snap-dragons and sunflowers, and nasturtians . . ."

Nastrutiums? Didn't Tolkien mean nasturtiums? That's exactly what his editors wanted to know back in 1954 when they were preparing the first volume of *The Lord of the Rings* trilogy for publication. Tolkien stood by the less common spelling. The ornamental in question had become a fixture of the English cottage garden, which is to say it was as ordinary and unpretentious, as "English," as Bilbo Baggins. "Nasturtian" was the anglicized version of the flower's early, and highly erroneous, Latin name.

But Tolkien did not dismiss the proofreader's concern out of hand; he first consulted the college gardener on the subject. Nasturtium, both scholar and gardener agreed, was the watercress, whereas, *Tropaeolum* was the proper Latin designation for the Indian cress or nasturtian. In the end, the editors let Tolkien have his way, as they did with such other now-treasured Tolkienisms as "elven," "dwarvish" and "eleventy-first." And so was the cheerful nasturtian allowed to make its appearance "peeping in at the round windows" at Bag End.

Presumably, hobbits grow nasturtiums (I will use the more common spelling henceforward) for the same reason that men do: because they look pretty.

The cultivars we admire in hanging baskets and garden borders are the descendants of both *Tropaeolum minus* and *Tropaeolum majus*, the first two species to reach the Old World from the New. In the 1800s, even more species were added to the mix by intrepid plant hunters tramping the higher reaches of the Andes. Thanks to them, we can now brighten our beds with anything from a straw-colored "Tom Thumb" to a vermilion "Empress of India."

Today, we know the nasturtium as both a creeper (think of the gravel paths at Monet's gardens at Giverny) and a climber (up lampposts and round the open windows of hobbit holes). In the eighteenth-century English garden, however, there were only climbers: the showy, round-leafed *T. majus* and the more bashful, yellow-flowered *T. minus*. By 1797, *T. majus* had become so popular that it almost drove *T. minus* out of business. Little *T. minus* owed its survival to the enthusiasm of one Dr. James Edward Smith, who pressed the seeds on all his friends and acquaintances.

A decade before this, Dr. Smith had bought the papers of famed Swedish botanist Carolus Linnaeus. It was Linnaeus who renamed the Indian cress *Tropaeolum* after the flowers' and leaves' resemblance, in his mind, to helmets and shields. To the ancient Greeks and Romans, of whom Linnaeus and his colleagues were so fond, the helmet and shield of a slain enemy were displayed as a trophy or *Tropaeolum* in Latin.

That said, we will now follow the botanist's eldest daughter, Elisabeth Cristina, on a late night ramble round her father's extensive flower beds. *T. majus* usually starts blooming in July. The Sun sets very late in Sweden in July, and Lisa Stina, as she was known to the family, required semidarkness for the observation she was about to make.

Like her sisters, Lisa Stina was forbidden to attend school, learn French, or follow fashion. Under such prohibitions, one can hardly blame the girl if she started imagining things. Though she never attended school, she was nevertheless erudite. When she was nineteen, she submitted a paper titled "Remarks on the Winking of the Indian Cress" to the Royal Swedish Academy of Sciences. (Even Lisa Stina was not sold on the name *Tropaeolum*!)

The paper described the electrical sparks she observed issuing from the flowers at dusk. It was not a shower of sparks, such as Gandalf might have conjured, but a spontaneous and intermittent phenomenon. The botanist's daughter established something of a fashion for observing the sparks: the poets Goethe and Erasmus Darwin claimed to have seen them, as did a handful of earnest scientists and philosophers of the day. Perhaps the thoughtful folk of the eighteenth century had gifts of perception that we have lost. Perhaps they simply had more imagination. Either way, what better excuse for a summer garden party than to watch for the mysterious "winking of the Indian cress?"

We don't know if Lisa Stina ever tasted her father's *Tropaeolum*. We do know that the ongoing confusion between Indian cress and watercress can be laid at the feet of horticulturist John Tradescant, who christened the newcomer *Nasturtium indicum* in 1656. (Contrary to popular belief, Linnaeus did not invent the system of classification; he organized and expanded it.) Previously, "nasturtium" had referred only to the watercress, a plant eaten as a green leafy since ancient times. To the Romans, it was *nasetortium*, or "nose-twister," for the peppery scent and taste of the leaves. The leaves of the Indian cress had a similar taste.

Despite the attention it received in John Evelyn's *Discourse of Sallets* (1699), the Indian cress never really got off the ground as a salad green. This is probably because the English at that time were not big salad eaters. (No lady in Queen Anne's court was ever heard to say, "Just a sallet for me!") Though the seed pods would be pickled and eaten like capers up through World War II, the Indian cress had established itself principally as an ornamental rather than a kitchen herb.

Old Flower Gets New Name in New World

Before it was pinned down as either *Tropaeolum* or *Nasturtium*, this New World native acquired a new name from just about every nurseryman who planted the seeds. No helmets for seventeenth-century herbalist John Parkinson; he called it "Yellow Larks' Heels." This was the yellow-flowered *T. minus*, the first species to arrive in Europe. Dr. Nicholas Monardes, on the other hand, called it *Flor de la Sangre*, translated into English in 1577 as "Floures of Blood."

Monardes, a physician residing in Seville, was not interested in the gold or jewels for which the Spanish court were so wild. What excited him were all the exciting new flora the New World had to offer. The seeds he procured from a home-bound Spanish caravel came directly from that part of "the Indies" known as "the Peru." The yellow flowers of *T. minus* are splashed with purple or red, hence, his bloody name for them.

Nasturtiums are still sometimes known in Spanish as *flor de la sangre*, but they are more commonly called "capuchina" after an entirely different sort of headgear than Linnaeus had in mind. It was that of the Capuchin monks, whose habits were characterized by the capuche, a long, pointed hood. In fact, outside the English-speaking world, this is the impression that has stuck. In French, the nasturtium is capucine, in Italian, *capuccina*, and in German, *Kapuzinerkresse*. (As far as this author is concerned, the nasturtium flower looks a lot more like Gandalf's hat than like any monk's hood or warrior's helmet!)

Of course, the nasturtium long predates the presence of both conquistadors and Capuchins in "the Peru." It is in the Andes that we find the most species of *Tropaeolum*: eighty-five at least. Among them are *T. peregrinum*, which adorned the walls of Inca palaces, the flame-flowered, blue-berried *T. speciosum*, and *T. polyphyllum*, which hardly looks like a nasturtium at all. *T. azuleum*, the blue nasturtium, is the gift the

Andes is keeping for itself: it has never been successfully propagated outside Chile.

T. tuberosum, known as "anu" or "mashua" in Quechua, was grown as a food crop long before the rise of the Inca Empire. Anu's orange and yellow flowers are pretty enough, but its real value lies under the soil. The tubers are still grown and eaten by farmers living in the high Andes. Rich in vitamin C, anu is usually eaten by women and children, sometimes cooked with molasses.

Legends and Myths

With such a long history, one would expect a legend or two to have come down to us from the days of the Inca or even before. Do an Internet search for a "legend of the nasturtium," however, and you will probably be directed to Isadora Newman's 1926 book, *The Legend of the Lilac and Other Fairy Flowers*. At twenty-eight pages, the book is, thankfully, as thin as it is disappointing. One can only wonder why Newman, supposedly a collector of folktales, chose to fabricate the stories in her book rather than track down the real thing. "A Legend of the Nasturtium" is a nauseatingly didactic faux fairy tale that has nothing to do with oral tradition and nothing to do with Peru.

For the real thing, or something close to it, we turn to Vernon Quinn's 1939 collection, *Stories and Legends of Garden Flowers*. Under the heading "Nasturtium," we find the story of Juan, a Quechua living in Peru at the time of the Spanish conquest. Though nominally Christian, Juan and his fellows persist in worshipping the old gods in secret. In order to refurbish the Mountain God's temple, which the Spaniards have plundered, Juan visits a nearby stream and scoops up a sackful of gold nuggets.

Our hero is headed to the village goldsmith with his haul when his luck runs out. Three Spanish soldiers waylay him on the trail. The most obnoxious of the three is a man named Martinez. Getting down from his horse, Martinez beats poor Juan, grabs the sack, and discovers the gold.

Of course, Martinez wants more. But rather than reveal his source, Juan beseeches the Mountain God to take the gold back. Spooked, the Spaniard's horse rears, throwing off the confiscated sack which lands in the underbrush. Martinez dives in after it, only to be bitten by a poisonous snake. He dies on the spot.

One might expect his surviving companions to seize the gold, but there is no gold. When the nuggets spilled out of the sack, the Mountain God transformed them into "a riotous vine covered with gold-yellow flowers." Writing in 1939, Vernon Quinn would probably have us believe the flowers were those of *T. majus*, the most familiar species by that time. Given the setting of the story, however, they are more likely to have been the anu or *T. tuberosum*.

Quinn goes on to assure us that Juan recovered from his beating, collected yet another sack of nuggets and, in collaboration with the goldsmith, was able to adorn Mountain God's altar.

And why should we believe that this story, if not literally true, is at least in keeping with tradition? The god, the snake, and the stream are all clues. To this day, each discernible peak in the Andes has its own *tiu*, or mountain god. To some extent, the *tiu* is the mountain, and the mountain is the *tiu*. He (and sometimes she) can also take the form of a snake. Gold idols are all very well, but the best way to appease a *tiu* is with a human life. This constitutes the dark side of Andean religion. In Juan's story, the *tiu*, in the form of a snake, helps himself to the greedy Martinez. The snake or serpent, who moves in the same way as a mountain stream, has long been regarded as a bringer of rain, a commodity more precious than gold.

For some of us, the nasturtium has never completely lost its Andean mystique. Tolkien was aware of the flower's ancestry, noting in a letter that it came "from Peru, I think." In fact, Bilbo's "nasturtians" are one of a handful of New World anachronisms in an otherwise distinctly Old World body of work.

Bilbo's World Offers Clues

In his book *J. R. R. Tolkien: Author of the Century*, Tolkien scholar Tom Shippey attempts to place our hobbit somewhere in real time. Citing the use of pipe tobacco and the arrival of morning mail, he dates Bilbo to somewhere after 1837. Shippey concedes the silliness of such an exercise—Bilbo is, after all, not really English. Silly or not, let us apply the same parameters to determine just what variety of "nasturtians" might have been peeping in those round windows at Bag End.

Given a starting date of 1837, we can eliminate any pure strain of *T. minus*. Despite the efforts of Dr. Smith, the species had fallen out of favor again and was not to be found in England. *T. speciosum*, known also as Scottish flame thrower, presents itself as a candidate. But *T. speciosum* does best with cool moisture and even a little bit of shade, whereas Bilbo's plants are growing in or near the same bed as his sunflowers and snapdragons. So we will restrict ourselves to varieties of *T. majus*.

The "Tom Thumb" variety appeared at the right time and comes in all colors, including Tolkien's "red and golden." But "Tom Thumb" is a mounder, not a climber—in other words, no peeping in the windows.

The year 1837 coincides with the coronation of Queen Victoria. From 1876 until her death, she was also Empress of India. As such, she was the namesake of another variety of *T. majus*. The deep red Empress of India arrived on the scene in 1884, well within Bilbo's "lifetime." It would have enjoyed the west-facing location assigned to it in Fellowship and would happily have trailed "all over the turf walls" of Bilbo's hobbit hole.

We should keep in mind, however, that Tolkien was a philologist, not a horticulturist. The flowers his imagination planted at Bag End were probably the same as he saw growing outside his own study in Oxford. So let's not confine ourselves to the Victorian era. *The Hobbit* was published in 1937, but "nasturtians" are not mentioned until *The Fellowship of the Ring* in 1954. Thus, when Sam Gangee took over care of the garden for Bilbo's nephew, Frodo, he would also have had the "Golden Gleam," "Scarlet Gleam," "Whirlybird," "Jewel," and "Gem" varieties to choose from. Actually, because many seed catalogs refer to all nasturtiums as "heirloom" varieties, it's hard to know which are the real antiques.

So, if you really want to reconstruct Bilbo's garden at Bag End (director Peter Jackson did it with what appear to be "Spitfire" and "Peach Melba"), just use your imagination. For my part, I've always been better at identifying flowers than growing them. Even more fun is naming them. In fact, if I could ever get *T. azuleum*, that tricky blue nasturtium, to grow on my doorstep, I would rechristen it "Gandalf's Hat." I might even throw it a little party at which my guests and I could sit quietly and watch for signs of winking.

Resources

Carpenter, Humphrey, ed. *The Letters of J. R. R. Tolkien*. Boston, MA: Houghton Mifflin Company, 1981.

Cook, Ferris. *The Garden Trellis: Designs to Build and Vines to Cultivate*. New York, NY: Artisan, a division of the Workman Publishing Company, 1996.

Gardner, Jo Ann. *The Heirloom Garden*. Pownal, VT: Storey Communications, Inc., 1992.

Hollingsworth, Buckner. *Flower Chronicles*. Rahway, NJ: Rutgers, the State University, 1958.

National Research Council. *Lost Crops of the Incas: Little-Known Plants of the Andes with Promise for Worldwide Cultivation*. Washington, DC: National Academy Press: 1989.

Perry, Frances. *Flowers of the World*. New York, NY: Galahad Books, 1972.

Quinn, Vernon. *Stories and Legends of Garden Flowers*. New York, NY: Frederick A. Stokes Company, 1939.

Shippey, Tom. *J. R. R. Tolkien: Author of the Century*. Boston, MA: Houghton Mifflin Company, 2001.

Tolkien, *J. R. R.. The Fellowship of the Ring*. New York, NY: Quality Paperback Book Club by arrangement with Houghton Mifflin, Inc., 1995.

Tale of the Cattail

⇌ by Susan Pesznecker ⇌

The sight of the tall cattail with its characteristic spike rising from pond or lake seems as much an obvious part of the outdoor gestalt as finding cactus on the desert sands. And indeed, the common cattail—*Typha capensis*, also known as *Typha latifolia*—is probably one of the most visually familiar plants on our planet, as well as one of the most widely dispersed. The word *Typha* comes from the Greek *tufh*, which translates as "bulrush." *Typha* may also refer to the puff of smoke-like appearance that takes place when the seed head opens and releases a flurry of down. *Capensis* is a Latin word meaning "broad leaf," referencing the cattail's thick, long leaves. A close relative is *Typha augustifolia*, the North American cattail.

The cattail family has a history rich in lore, magic, and ethnobotany. These are plants that have long been used as foodstuffs and for a multitude of homely purposes by most aboriginal tribes. Within the ecosystem, cattails furnish a rich habitat for plants and animals and also provide an important cleansing function in their ability to purify water and stabilize wetlands.

Botanical Details

The cattail is an erect, rhizomatous, semi-aquatic or aquatic perennial herb. In other words, it grows straight and tall and spreads underground by advancing root-like structures. In some undisturbed ecosystems, a vast area can be covered in cattails that are actually a single plant. Cattails always grow in water, typically in boggy wetlands or on the edges of lakes and ponds. Because the rhizomes are underwater and isolated from temperature changes and surface fires, the plants are extremely hardy. Cattails are perennial, dying back in the fall and reappearing in the spring. They're a disturbance-loving species, moving quickly into areas disturbed by excavation, deforestation, or dredging.

The cattail is easy to identify visually, because of its long, thin stalk and familiar spike. The spike actually contains two components: an elongated brown "male" seed head atop a greenish tubular "female" ovule. Both seed head and ovule contain minute flowers; when these bloom, they erupt into a thick burst of cottony fluff that is dispersed on the wind. Cattail stems may reach ten feet in an ideal setting. At the base of the plant, thin, elongated grayish-green leaves gather sunlight.

Cattails are found in most parts of the world, including the equatorial regions and just about everywhere but the Artic and Antarctica. Besides spreading vegetatively through rhizomes, they also reproduce through dispersing of seeds: a single cattail spike may produce more than 250,000! The spike bursts into fluff during late summer or early fall, sending its seeds into the air. When the seeds hit water, their protective coating dissolves and they immediately sink, take root, and grow. Germination rates are high and occur within a wide range of temperatures and moisture. Once growth begins, rhizomes form quickly and growth accelerates.

Ethnobotany

Botanist Euell Gibbons once called cattails "the supermarket of the swamp," which hints at the versatility of this plant.

To begin with, cattail has a number of food uses. In early spring, the 2- to 3-foot-high shoot can be cut, peeled, and cooked like asparagus. The male pollen head produces a copious amount of yellow pollen early in the growth cycle; this may be used like flour. Early in spring, the roots may be prepared like any tuberous vegetable and eaten "as is." The roots may also be harvested, dried, and pounded into root starch, creating a substance useful for thickening or making gruels or puddings. Cattail spikes can be roasted and eaten like ears of corn.

Cattails have served as structural materials through a number of cultures. The stalks were used to thatch walls and roofs and were bundled to create rafts. The leaves were woven into ground cloths, canoe sails, mats, roofing materials, and clothing, while the down was used to stuff bedding and as absorbent padding for diapers and menstrual aids. Fiber from the stalks was formed into ropes and pounded into rudimentary paper. Stalks, leaves, and down were used to create animal fat torches, while the down alone made a quick fire starter.

Medicinal Uses

The roots of cattail may be split, macerated, and applied directly to minor burns, insect bites, and simple wounds. Cattail leaves may be dried, burned, and the ash used as both an antiseptic and styptic agent. Milking young leaves—pulled from the plant base—produces a few drops of antiseptic liquid that can be applied directly to wounds. Cattail down makes an absorbent dressing and can be used as a poultice.

In some North American Indian tribes, sleeping on a mat woven from cattail leaves was a treatment for cysts and various orthopedic conditions.

Magic and Lore

In British English, the cattail is often called a bulrush (bull rush), although from a botanical standpoint, the bulrush is an entirely different species of plant. The plant is also known as reedmace in the United Kingdom, presumably because the plant resembles a medieval mace. Regional American nicknames include "punk" (as in the long match-like stick used to light fuses), "soft flag," and (in the southern United States) "corndog grass."

The Gaelic language calls the cattail *cuigeal nam ban-sìdh*, which means "the great reed mace." Legend says that Jesus held a reed mace in his hand when he was struck down by Roman soldiers, and suggests that the vinegar-soaked sponge was extended to him using a reed mace extension.

According to Daniel Moerman, professor of anthropology at the University of Michigan, cattail leaves were commonly used by Cheyenne tribes in the annual Sun Dance ceremony, while the Navaho people used a whole-plant preparation as a ritual emetic.

In magickal terms, the cattail is a decidedly masculine plant and is often referenced as both a solar and a phallic symbol. Both AJ Drew, author of *A Wiccan Formulary and Herbal*, and Wiccan author Scott Cunningham assign the cattail to a fire correspondence; I also find that it has pronounced qualities of air, given its lofty stalk and tall habitus, as well as the way the cattail releases its seeds into the sky as so much aerated fluff. If you're ever doing ritual in the outdoors and find that you lack a few key tools, a freshly snipped cattail stem makes a fabulous wand and even a decent sword.

In addition to fire and air, one could argue that the cattail shares a water correspondence, given its choice of habitat. Its effectiveness at environmental cleanup (see below) also gives it serious credibility as an earth correspondence and makes the cattail one of those rare plants that spans the four elementals.

Environmental Benefits

Cattail is one of the first aquatic plants to colonize newly exposed mud in raw wetlands and is also a key player in the process by which open water is first converted to wetland, then to bog, and finally to "dry" land. Cattail's tenacity and rapid growth combine to make it one of the highest biomass producers of any living plant. As perennial plants, cattails shed their leaves, stems, and flowers each year, creating a regular load of plant debris. This debris decomposes rapidly and creates a layer that adds to the straining and purification abilities of the cattail-dominated ecosystem. Water percolates through the dense layers of plant matter and rhizome and is effectively purified. Cattails are very tolerant to organic toxins, oils, and heavy metals like lead, zinc, copper, and nickel; the plants are not harmed by these substances and are able to clear them effectively from the water. A recent experiment investigated cattail as a cheap, simple way to remove arsenic from drinking water (Graham).

Cattail-dominated wetlands provide valuable habitat for wildlife, including fish, eels, birds, insects, and some mammals. Muskrats and beavers use cattails to construct their lodges, which also provide shelter for fish and resting spots for birds and insects. Geese, muskrats, and nutria eat the cattail rhizomes, and some birds eat the seeds. Deer and other animals hide in the cattails, using them for protective cover. Many birds nest within the cattails, including the red-winged blackbird, yellow-headed blackbird, and marsh wren.

Honoring the Plant

The cattail has a unique appearance and demonstrates spectacular versatility in its uses and potential functions. Next time you pass a stand of cattails, stop for a moment and contemplate what you're looking at. Be aware of the animal life within the tall stems. Visualize what's happening beneath your view, as these plants sweeten the soil and water surrounding them. Pause and honor the cattail, which has stood tall for millennia and knows exactly how to do what it does best.

Resources

Cameron, John. *Gaelic Names of Plants, Scottish and Irish, with Notes*. Edinburgh: Blackwood and Sons, 1883. Google Books.

Cunningham, Scott. *Encyclopedia of Magical Herbs*. St. Paul, MN: Llewellyn, 1997.

Drew, AJ. *A Wiccan Formulary and Herbal*. Franklin Lakes, NJ: New Page, 2005.

Gibbons, Euell. *Stalking the Wild Asparagus*. Putney, VT: Alan C. Hood and Company, 1962.

Graham, Michael. "Inexpensive Arsenic Filtration System Based on Cattails Could Help Clean Up the Drinking Water of 57 Million People." Treehugger.com/ http://tinyurl.com/4efludb.

Moerman, Daniel. *Native American Medicinal Plants. An Ethnobotanical Dictionary*. Portland, OR: Timber Press, 2009.

Herbs, Healers & Charms

⤜ by Sharynne MacLeod NicMhacha ⤛

In traditional Celtic communities, there were special healers known as "fairy seers" or "fairy doctors." They were said to be able to see the fairies and knew how to help others in their interactions with them. Fairy doctors could tell if a particular disease had a natural cause or if it was caused by the fairies. If the illness had a natural cause, the fairy doctor might prescribe herbs or other remedies. If it was due to the fairies, they would prescribe charms or other rituals. Some fairy doctors would only deal with fairy-related issues. If a disease was naturally caused, they would indicate to the patient that it had nothing to do with their business, and would refer them to a doctor or herbalist.

Some healers and seers spent time in the Otherworld, where they received skills or powers. Many fairy doctors were paid with gifts or food, rather than money. They were extremely careful not to upset or disrespect the fairies in their work. Some fairy doctors did not work with herbs, but only with charms. Others used hazel rods, butter, water from holy wells, and sacred stones.

One of the most famous Irish folk healers was Biddy Early, a woman who lived in County Clare and died in 1874. She used a glass bottle, which was said to have been given to her by the fairies (or in other accounts, by the spirit of her deceased son or husband). When people arrived at her door, Biddy would know their name, where they came from, and why they had come. She would look into her bottle with one eye, keeping the other eye open. In this way she perceived information about illnesses or other problems the person might have, whether present or in the future. Biddy Early prescribed herbs and healing rituals for her clients, as well as magical and protective ceremonies. Some of her prescriptions would provide direct healing, while others were intended to help with problems with the unseen realms.

Folk healers and seers also were found in Scotland. They too worked with herbs, stones, and sacred water. Many charms and prayers have been recorded which were recited in order to provide physical or spiritual healing. Some of these prayers invoked the elements of the natural world. In addition to prayers, folk healers also used songs and chants, and performed healing with the breath and distance healing.

To cure sprains, Scottish folk healers used a technique known as *Eólas an Sguchaidh*, which means "the Knowledge of the Charm of the Sprain." An extract of St. John's wort was rubbed on the sprained area while a long invocation was recited by the healer. The continual recitation of the charm was frequently interrupted by small emissions of breath released between the teeth. A flaxen cord called a "tolm" was knotted three times and then passed through the healer's mouth during the healing. In other cases, the cord was left inside the healer's mouth during the performance of the cure.

In Scotland there were many charms and rituals used to work with invisible spirits or forces. The removal or counteracting of the evil eye was often performed in the Highlands. In one such prayer, the healer loudly invoked a list of powers she or he possessed, which could counteract this type of malicious intentions or energies. Among these were the powers of wind, fire, thunder, lightning, storm, Moon, Sun and stars. One female healer said that the minute she began her chanting she knew whether the person's condition was due to natural causes or to the evil eye. The healer remarked that the evil eye sent by a man was more difficult to counteract than of a woman. The man's was more powerful, evidently, but the woman's was more venomous.

Certain Scottish folk seers and healers were renowned for having special knowledge of the Fairy folk. These practitioners were considered experts in making offerings or performing rituals to correct or maintain a good relationship with the inhabitants of the Otherworld. Neil Beaton of the Isle of Skye was the doctor to MacLeod of Dunvegan. Although his cures were reputed to have been learned from the devil (i.e., the non-Christian powers of the Otherworld), he was in great demand all over the Highlands and Islands.

Many types of herbs were used utilized in traditional Scottish and Irish healing magic, rites, and invocations. Herbal charms and spells were used to obtain good fortune, health, friendship, joy, love, abundance, victory, confidence, and protection. Herbal magic was a common method for overcoming or protecting against malice, envy, fear, falsehood, ill luck, fraud, oppression, scarcity, bad news, and the evil eye. Herbal cures and charms were also used to provide physical healing through the physical properties of the plant or through its magical or spiritual properties.

Some plants could only be used if they appeared in your path unbidden or unsought. Some herbs were gathered during high tide rather than ebb tide. Others were collected or prepared during particular phases of the moon. Many charms refer to special traditions or prophecies that were known to the healer which specified how the plant was to be used or what attributes it possessed. Magical charms were often recited just before or during the culling of the plant. Others were to be used while the plant was applied.

An Irish Herbal

In Ireland, many types of herbs were used by folk healers and fairy doctors. These included (in alphabetical order): apple, bedstraw, black knapweed, bog bine, bog-myrtle, burdock, chamomile, cleavers, clover, daisy, dandelion, docken, fern, flax, groundsel, hazel, ivy, juniper, lichen, loose-strife, mugwort, mullein, nettles, oak bark, ox-tongue herb, pennywort, plantain, primrose, quince, roses, rowan, tansy, vervain, water buttercup, watercress, woodbine, and yarrow.

Healing herbs were frequently boiled in water and then ingested for healing or other benefits. Charming herbs were also sometimes burned in a flame or used with conjunction with sacred water.

There were special times at which herbs were gathered or utilized, and there were also particular methods used to gather or administer them. Some herbs had to be lifted from the soil in three pulls. Others were not to be gathered while the wind was shifting. In Ireland, wild chamomile was known as the "Father of All Herbs" or the "Father of the Ground," and was culled only with a black-handled knife. Mullein was believed to have the ability to return children who had been taken by the fairies. A small amount of mullein taken every day in an herbal blend was believed to bestow long life.

One Irish healer said that when he was looking for the right cure, he would bend down on his knees and say a prayer to the king and the queen of the fairies before gathering a plant. If there were pale or blackened leaves on the plant, he knew that the illness was caused by the fairies. If the plant was fresh and clear, he knew the illness was not caused by them and would be suitably treated with a natural or physical remedy.

Another healer said that when he prepared an herbal cure for a male patient, when he gathered the necessary herb he called out the name of a man other than his patient and referred to him as a king (*rí*). If the cure was for a woman, the name of another woman was spoken aloud and referred to as a queen (*ban-ríon*). The healer explained that this was a method of calling upon the king or queen of the plant itself.

In Irish tradition, certain magical or healing practices, including the methods of gathering and utilizing sacred plants, were often attributed to the gifts and influence of the Fairy Folk. One report about the use of mullein, or *lus-mor*, the "Great Herb" or plant, said that if the wind changed direction while the healer was cutting it, the cutter would go mad. In addition, if the healer was paid for performing the cure, they could gather the plant whenever they wished. However, if they were not paid, the fairies might not like it.

One Irish healer stated that she used *slan-lus* (plantain) and *garb-lus* (dandelion) to revive those who had died. However, she also stated that she could not heal all conditions, including anyone who had received the "fairy stroke" from the Queen or Fool of the fairies. She used a wide variety of herbs, including knapweed, tansy, wild chamomile, water buttercup, and lichen. Knapweed was boiled with other herbs in water with a bit of sugar and administered for pains in the bones. Water buttercup was also used for the bones. Tansy was boiled and used for heart conditions. Lichen was used to treat the heart. Loosestrife was believed to keep all bad things away.

Another healer said that dandelion was an herb used for all conditions that had to do with the fairies. If a preparation of the plant was taken by the patient for conditions pertaining to the fairies, it would either cure them or kill them on the spot. In another report, a woman healer said that there were two types of dandelion: the white, which "had no harm in it" and the red, which had a *pishogue* (fairy spell) in it. She said that she traditionally left the red type alone.

A female herbal healer from Ireland said that Monday and Tuesday were good days for gathering herbs, but not on Sunday, for on that day there "was no cure." She also used lichen for heart conditions. Ribgrass was used to reduce lumps. It had to be taken in three pulls or the healer would "lose one's head" (i.e., go mad). It was warmed on the tongs from the fire and then placed on the lump that was being treated.

A woman healer from Slieve Echtga said she prescribed wild parsnip for gravel (kidney stones) and felt there was no plant so effective for regulating the heartbeat as dandelion. She also used a plant called *Miona madar* (madder), which she described as having little blue flowers on it. A preparation of this plant was used to cure running sores and other conditions. The charm to be recited while gathering the plant had in it the name of an "old curer or magician," and was spoken three times and then breathed into a piece of tow (flax or hemp fiber prepared for spinning). This was then placed on the person to be cured, and the healer herself felt this was a very good cure. However, she suggested only using this cure for oneself or someone close to you, but not for a stranger. This was because the fairies "know all things," including who are performing these charms. Therefore, she felt it was of no good purpose to put oneself in danger unnecessarily.

A male healer from the west of Ireland recommended using ivy that grew on a whitethorn bush to make cures for bad eyes. He also said that if a person cut a hazel rod and brought it with them, turning it around them now and again, no bad thing could harm them.

A Scottish Herbal

In the late nineteenth and early twentieth centuries, folklorists and collectors gathered a great deal of very specific traditional knowledge and lore in the Highlands and Islands of Scotland pertaining to herbal cures and traditional healers. Many of these reports contain information about magical herbs, charms, and prayers as well.

In one charm for gathering yarrow, the healer states that the plant is being gathered so that his or her hand will be more brave, their foot more swift, and their speech like the beams of the sun. In another folk prayer, the charmer prays to be like an island in the ocean, a hill on the shore, a star in the waning moon, and a rock in the sea. In one charm used to counter urinary infection in cattle from the Highlands, the healer faced the rising Sun and intoned a prayer that invoked the powers of the sea and the water of the nine wells of the god Mannanán mac Lir.

A number of plants were used in folk healing rituals in Scotland. These included (in alphabetical order): bramble, bog myrtle, bog violet, catkins, club moss, dandelion, fairy wort, fern seed, figwort, ivy, juniper, mistletoe, orpin (stone crop), passion flower, pearlwort, primrose, purple orchis, red-stalk, reeds, Saint John's wort, shamrock, vervain, watercress, and yarrow.

Saint John's wort was called "the noble yellow plant," and was widely used to ward off the malicious use of second sight or enchantment, evil eye, or death. It was also believed to grant wishes, ensure victory in battle, encourage fertility and abundance, and bestow good luck, peace, plenty, and prosperity.

Yarrow was only effective if it was found without seeking it. Traditionally, it was gathered with the right hand and preserved with the left. When the yarrow was encountered, it was secretly placed inside a woman's bodice or under a man's vest on the left side, while the lucky recipient recited a traditional charm. It was believed to bestow spiritual or magical power, and was often used in divination rites.

Bog violet was used to promote safe childbirth, provide protection while traveling, bring wisdom and eloquence, and overcome harm and the evil eye. In one charm for gathering bog violet, the healer refers to the herb as the most precious plant in the field. Gathering bog violet ensured that the healer would have the eloquence and wisdom of "the seven priests." Bog violet was frequently used in love spells. The woman who performed the love spell would gather nine roots of the bog violet while she rested on her left knee. The roots of the plant were then knotted together to form a ring. The ring was placed inside the mouth of the young woman who desired the spell. If she managed to kiss a particular man while the ring was still inside her mouth he would fall in love with her forever (as long as he was unaware of her using the ring).

Figwort was called the plant of "a thousand blessings." It had numerous medicinal uses, and was used to treat cuts, bruises, and sores. Figwort was also utilized to ensure an abundant supply of milk. It also had a number of magical applications. Figwort was traditionally gathered during the flowing tide, as it was associated with the flowing or releasing of milk or water (as well as general abundance). The plant was perceived to bring a person joy, love, peace, and power.

Juniper was used to provide protection against misfortune, fear, danger or fatigue. It was traditionally burned in the house and barn on New Year's morning in Scotland as a purifying incense. In order to harness its protective powers, the juniper plant was pulled up by its roots with its branches formed into four bundles. The bundles rested between the five fingers, while a traditional charm was recited.

The purple orchis was often used in love spells. It has two roots, one of which is larger than the other, which represented a man and a woman. The purple orchis had to be pulled up by its roots before dawn while the person gathering the plant stood facing the south. The plant was then placed in a vessel of water, taking care that no hint of the sun was visible above the horizon. If the plant sank in the water, the person whose love was desired would in fact become the person's partner. The love charm could be made in a more general way as well, without naming a specific lover. In this form of the spell, the roots of the purple orchis were dried and the powder was placed underneath one's pillow to invoke prophetic dreams of your future partner.

The shamrock was a plant that also had to be found without searching for it. As is widely known, the four or five-leafed clover was an invincible talisman. This plant was frequently referred to as the "shamrock of blessings" or the "shamrock of power." It was associated with good omens, as well as "the seven joys," which are: health, friends, cattle, sheep, sons, daughters, peace, and connection with the sacred.

Ivy was associated with fertility and bounty, including abundance of milk and the fruitful bringing forth of calves. On the Quarter Days (Imbolc, Beltaine, Lugnasad, and Samhain), young women pinned three leaves of ivy onto their nightgowns to bring on dreams of their future partners.

Catkin fiber was used in herbal and magical charms to ensure or increase the abundance of milk and herds. It was also utilized for protection against the loss of animals or other means of survival, to bring about success, and even to protect against the loss of friends.

In traditional charms, club moss was believed to provide powerful protection from harm or mishap, and could ensure safety during travel, even during the dark. It was said that no harm could befall a person if club moss was in their path.

Fairy wort had the power to overcome all oppression, and as its name implies, this power was believed to have its origin in the fairy realms. This esteemed plant repelled scandal, hatred, falsehood, fraud, bad luck, ill love or a bad life, for the entire length of a person's existence.

The root of Queen Anne's lace (or wild carrot) were gathered at Michaelmas with a special three-pronged spade. Each woman sang an incantation while gathering the roots of the plant, which ensured her fertility and abundance. To find a forked carrot was considered an auspicious omen and signified that the woman would be the recipient of extremely powerful fertility forces. The carrots were washed, then tied up in small bunches with red thread and put in small pits near the home. The carrots were then covered with sand.

Combinations of herbs were also used in herbal and healing charms. Protective wreaths were made from ivy, rowan, and either bramble or honeysuckle. Small wreaths of milkwort, butterwort, dandelion, and marigold, about three or four inches in diameter and bound by a triple cord of flax, were placed underneath milk vessels in order to prevent the fairies from stealing the essence of the milk. A combination of trefoil, vervain, St. John's wort and dill was said to "hinder witches in their will" (i.e., protect against malicious or non-beneficial influences).

In early Celtic tradition, the Otherworld was considered to be the source of wisdom, skill, power, guidance, and protection, as well as healing and transformation. Well into the last century, many traditional folk healers and seers, including herbal healers and fairy doctors, were reported to have received their wisdom of herbal cures and their powers of healing directly from the Celtic Otherworld itself.

World of Ethnobotany

～ by Susan Pesznecker ～

In the Pacific Northwest, where I hail from, the indigenous First People that I know prefer the title of "Indian" to "Native American." I honor this use.
~ Susan Pesznecker

"Ethno" is a prefix referring to the study of culture or ethnicity, while "botany" is the study of plants. Ethnobotany, therefore, is an investigation into how plants and plant materials are used by traditional cultures and ethnic groups, or—more specifically—about the relationships that develop between people and plants. When we study ethnobotany, we explore what people have come to understand

about plants, and how they interact with them. Combined with botanical science, this helps us understand more about plants and about our ecosystem.

The idea of ethnobotany has been with us for as long as humans have used plants, and the written record of herbalism dates back to at least 3000 BCE, with the Sumerians recording the medicinal use of such common plants as laurel, caraway, and thyme. Theophrastus' *Historia Plantarum*, written in the fourth century BCE, is said to be a defining work in launching the study of botany, while many of the ancient formularies—such as Dioscorides' *Materia Medica* and Galen's *De Simplicibus*—were early examples of recorded ethnobotany.

During the Middle Ages, roughly 400–1500 CE and usually defined as the period between Greek and Roman culture and the Renaissance, herbalism made progress as both craft and science. Interest in herbalism, botany, and ethnobotany was demonstrated by the hundreds of formularies and herbals written by hand or published after the invention of the printing press in the fifteenth century. Theophrastus' *Historia* was one of the first books to be printed, with Dioscorides' *Materia* not far behind. But the sixteenth and seventeenth centuries saw a steady erosion of respect for cultural and ethnic uses of plants. The advent of physical and empirical sciences led to a science-dominated worldview that persisted well into the 1800s and 1900s.

The earliest ethnobotanical studies were conducted separately by cultural anthropologists and botanists in the 1800s; working independently, they didn't share findings outside of their own spheres. It was only when they began to collaborate around 1900 that the field took root. As a formal discipline, the term "ethnobotany" was coined in 1895 by United States botanist John William Harshberger. The twentieth century found ethnobotany shifting from simple data collection and observation to methodological and conceptual organization. Today, academic ethnobotany requires knowledge of botany, cultural and practical anthropology, linguistics, and training in herbal and naturalist skills. Much information about the traditional uses of plants still rests with aboriginal "First Peoples," who may or may not choose to share their knowledge with outsiders. Much remains to be discovered.

Worlds of Ethnobotany

Whether used for construction, fabrics, plant dyes, baskets, food, currency, sacred purpose, healing, or a myriad of other uses for plants, ethnobotany opens windows to the past and enlightens the present as well. Here, for illustration, is a look at the ethnobotanical "history" of some common plants: pine, yucca, bush berries, sweet grass, and western red cedar.

Pine (Pinus)

More than 100 species of pine trees belong to the genus *Pinus*. The trees grow in most parts of the world but are especially prevalent in the northern hemisphere. Pines are evergreen and resinous; that is, they produce a dense resin which most know as "pitch." Foliage takes the form of needles, and seeds are borne in cones of various sizes, depending on species. Some seeds release at a certain age; other cones must be broken open by birds or only open when subjected to the heat from wildfires.

Pine trees grow quickly and produce useful softwood for construction. Indians gathered the needles to weave baskets and food containers. The split, dried roots were used to make ropes and fishing nets. The pitch—which exudes from bark lesions and hardens—made excellent fire starters.

Some *Pinus* species produce edible seeds known as pinyons or pine nuts; these are nutritious and oily, making them a quality food source. The inner cambium bark is rich in starch and vitamins A and D; it can be eaten raw or dried and powdered into starchy flour. The young, soft needles of some species can be brewed into a vitamin-rich tea.

Daniel Moerman, who teaches anthropology, notes that virtually every part of the pine tree has medicinal use. The powdered inner cambium was used to make a poultice for wounds and joint pain, while a cambium decoction worked as both diuretic and purgative. Pitch was used as an ointment base and burned as a fumigant to clear lungs and kill insect vermin. Infusions and decoctions of the pitch and resin had a wide range of uses, including treating tuberculosis, cough, and stomachache. The young needles were infused to treat nervous ailments and stomach disorders; they were also used as a skin wash for rashes and minor irritations. The powdered sap of some species treated eye disorders.

Pinus has sacred uses, too. Moerman reports that pitch was often combined with deer fat or bear tallow and applied to the body as a purifier following ritual or sweat baths. An infusion of *Pinus flexilis* was used as a ceremonial emetic, while hunters smoked the needles to bring luck. Smoke created by burning Eastern white pine needles was believed to drive away ghosts and spirits.

Yucca (Yucca)

The yucca is a perennial shrub or tree (the Joshua tree is a species of yucca) notable for its thick, sword-shaped leaves and central flower sprays or panicles. The forty-nine known species of yucca grow in arid and desert regions of Central, North, and South America, as well as the Caribbean. It was sometimes known as "Spanish sword," perhaps for its resemblance to the swords of Spanish explorers who explored the Americas. The plant is hardy and long-lived but dependent on mutualistic pollination by the yucca moth.

Many parts of the yucca were used for food, particularly by desert-dwelling Indians. Yucca's fruits, seeds, flowers, and flowering stems were edible, and some ate the roots as well. The flower stalks were boiled or roasted like asparagus. The fruit and flowers were eaten raw or cooked; the flowers were often bitter and best eaten before the blossoms developed fully. Yucca crowns and sap are rich in natural sugar and were used to produce alcoholic drinks. Couplan and Duke report that First Peoples in Mexico and what is now south Texas fermented yucca to create a drink known as *sotol*, which was sometimes distilled to increase the alcohol content further.

Yucca elata roots were used as a source for saponin, a soap-like plant, creating a shampoo for both everyday use and pre-ritual cleansing. Saponins were sometimes put into streams to stun and kill fish. The dried leaves were easily ignited and made an excellent medium for starting fires. Medicinally, crushed roots were used as poultices or brewed into infusions or decoctions for a number of maladies, particularly as a skin wash for rashes, boils, insect bites, etc. An infusion of young shoots was used to calm nerves and as a general tonic.

The roots were especially important for ritual and ceremonial use. Moerman notes that root infusions were used in purification baths and ceremonies, as a smudge ingredient, as a delirifacient (a drug that induces delirium), and—for the Cherokee—in conjunction with broom sedge and amaranth as part of their "green corn medicine".

Bush Berries: Blueberry, Cranberry, Huckleberry (Vaccinium)

Blueberries, cranberries, and huckleberries are members of genus *Vaccinium*. These berries were vital to many of the First Peoples as a food source and continue to be valued today. The plants are typically found in cooler regions of the northern hemisphere and often at moderate to high elevations as well. They require acidic soils and prefer heath and bog areas.

Blueberries were enjoyed as a seasonal food source and dried for later use in tea and pemmican. The berries would sometimes be mashed and dried into small cakes. Pojar and McKinnon note that all varieties of bush berries were sometimes preserved in animal or fish grease.

The fruit and leaves were widely used to treat gastrointestinal disorders, including nausea, vomiting, diarrhea, and infant colic. A leaf infusion was used as a skin wash and as a beverage and general tonic. Ceremonially, the infusion was drunk during rituals to insure prosperity and health. This is interesting in today's terms, as modern science now considers blueberry to be a "super food" containing powerful antioxidants and capable of improving memory, slowing the aging process, and fighting a number of diseases.

The cranberry is a low shrub that favors lowland acidic bogs in cool northern climes. Like blueberries, cranberries are known to be high in antioxidants. Fresh and dried cranberries were an important food source for the Indians living in proximity. Infusions of leaves and fruit were used to clean wounds and to treat digestive upsets and lung and kidney ailments. In today's times, pure cranberry juice is used as a urine acidifier to treat bladder infections.

The evergreen huckleberry is similar to the blueberry, but with fruit that is smaller, darker, and more tart. Huckleberries are found at moderate elevations on North America's west coast, following the same distribution as western red cedars. Huckleberries were prized as a food source and were used fresh, dried, in simple preserves, and in pemmican or dried cakes. The fruit of blueberries, cranberries, and huckleberries was widely used as a plant dye for fabrics and basketry materials. Infusions of roots, stems, leaves, and/or berries were used to treat joint disorders and lung disorders. Some species of huckleberry were used as abortifacients, inducing labor, bringing on menses, or speeding recovery after childbirth.

Ceremonially, huckleberries have a key role in the "First Salmon" feast given annually by the Indians of the Pacific Northwest's Columbia Plateau. In Celilo, Oregon, a ritual meal of salmon, venison, roots (camas and wapato), and huckleberries precedes a community feast (Pesznecker). This ritual is thought to be key to that season's hunting and fishing success. Note: If you head into the mountains to gather huckleberries, proceed with care: bears like them as much as humans do!

Sweet Grass (Hierochloe odorata)

Sweet grass is a tall, ordinary looking green grass that is widely dispersed throughout sunny climes in North America and Europe. It spreads by rhizome and forms dense groups of blades that may reach 24 inches. When picked, cut, or crushed, the leaves release a sweet vanilla scent that gives the grass its name. Many people describe the aroma as like "new-mown hay." The typical scent comes from coumarins (COO-murh-inns) within the plant. Coumarin is used in modern pharmacology as a precursor to the anticoagulant drug Coumadin.

The plant's botanical name, *Hierochloe odorata*, comes from Greek and means "fragrant holy plant." Sweet grass has a number of folk names as well, including bison grass, buffalo grass, holy grass (UK), manna grass, Mary's grass, seneca grass, and vanilla grass. Many of these names give hints at the lore and uses of sweet grass. Sweet grass is best harvested in midsummer; if left until the first frost, much of the scent is lost. Some users cut the grass close to the ground using a sharp blade, while others pull the grass by hand after discovering that this "tears" the rhizomes and actually increases the plant's future growth. A few aboriginal tribes braid the blades of grass before cutting, then cut the finished braids; this is done to honor the Earth Mother as it is believed that her hair (the grass) should not be torn from her head (the earth). The harvested leaves air-dry quickly and are bundled stored in dry form.

Many Indians in the United States regard sweet grass as a sacred herb. Its most important use is in ritual, where it is burned as incense or used in smudges intended to purify, protect, honor ancestors, or bring peace. Although the evidence remains anecdotal, many suggest sweet grass has psychotropic properties and may be chewed to induce a mild, meditative state.

Sweet grass has practical uses as well. Several blades were bundled to form paintbrushes and used to paint ceremonial tools, such as pipes and rattles. A number of tribes used the grass as a fragrant stuffing for pillows and mattresses, while others used the blades in basketry. Sweet grass was burned to repel mosquitoes and other insects. The blades were woven into the hair for adornment, and the dried leaves were used to create scented hair wash and a rudimentary perfume. For Plains Indians, sweet grass was so highly valued that it was used in trade as a form of currency.

The plant also had a number of medicinal uses. Smoke from the burning dried leaves was inhaled as treatment for colds and lung ailments. An infusion of sweet grass leaves was taken for coughs, colds, and venereal infections as well as to treat fever. Moerman reports that the Blackfoot and other Plains tribes used sweet grass to treat saddle sores on their horses and fed them leaves to fortify them for long rides.

Besides its modern pharmacological uses, sweet grass today is also used in Europe as a flavoring agent for various brands of soda—a modern take on ethnobotany.

Western Red Cedar (Thuja plicata)

Ethnobotanist Hilary Stewart notes, "So thoroughly did the cedar permeate the culture of the Northwest Coast peoples that it is hard to envision their life without it". Pojar and McKinnon likewise refer to cedars as "Trees of Life." A Coast Salish myth tells us that "Great Spirit created red cedar in honor of a man who will always be helping others. When he dies and where he is buried, a cedar tree will grow and be usefully to the people—the roots for baskets, the bark for clothing, the wood for shelter." Truly, cedar exemplifies a plant that served its culture in both practical and sacred ways.

The western red cedar is a massive tree that easily sur-
passes 200 feet in height and reach 14 feet in diameter. The
oldest verified western red cedar is estimated to be 1,460 years
old (Earle). The tree requires a wet, coastal climate and commonly grows on North America's west coast, from northern
California, along Oregon and Washington, along the Canadian
coast and up through Alaska's inland passage. The trees also
push east, but without a source of coastal moisture, they don't
reach the spectacular size of those growing near the ocean.

Cedar wood was split into planks and used to build long-
lasting structures, such as longhouses and storage containers. Whole cedar logs were felled for canoes and totem poles.
Small pieces of wood were carved into ornate bowls, cups,
utensils, masks, and other objects, while shavings were used
within dwellings in bedding and to discourage insects. Red
cedar wood was used to create fire for drying and smoking
fish. Not only did the wood impart a pleasant scent to the fish,
but the smoke was minimal.

Bark was used to make everything from clothing to baskets to ropes and threads. Cedar withes are long, thin twig-
like structures that hang from the tree's branches. Withes—
which have enormous tensile strength—and roots were used
to make rope and strong baskets.

Medicinally, cedar's needles and twigs were made into
infusions to treat cough, rheumatism, stomach pain, kidney trouble, and a number of other common disorders. The
needles were also powdered and mixed with fish oil to make
poultices for joint and stomach pain and bronchitis. The inner
bark was chewed to induce menstruation and labor. A decoction of boughs treated tuberculosis and cough and was also

used as a hair and skin wash. Although *Thuja plicata* was not an important food source, an infusion of needles provided a tasty resource for vitamins A and C and may have been used as a tonic.

Western red cedar has important ceremonial uses for Pacific Northwest coastal tribes. Wood was used to shape elaborate masks, ritual vessels, and other ceremonial items, all displaying spirit animals and clan crests. Cedar shavings were burned as a richly aromatic ritual incense. The tree itself is honored as a gift of the Creator and as something essential to the First Peoples' way of life.

Do You Want to Know More?

Are you interested in exploring ethnobotany further? I have three suggestions.

First, learn more about the plants around you—the plants in your yard, in your countryside, and in your state or region. You might find a website or a good book on the botany of your area—see my "Resources" list for a few ideas. Ethnobotany begins with getting curious. Poke around and see what you find. Discover what is growing along the roadside near your home or on the edges of your own yard. Delve into your own family history and think about how plants may have been used.

Second, look into phenology: the art and science of recurring natural phenomena. When you observe the trees losing their leaves in autumn, a creek's annual flooding, seasonal auroras borealis, birds flying south during the winter, or the first frost of the year, you're watching phenology in action. By studying and contemplating phenology, we learn more about the earth's natural cycles. In a slightly different, more complex, "hard-science" definition, phenology is defined as "a branch of science dealing with the relations between climate and periodic biological phenomena." Stated another way, phenology is the study of the response of living organisms to seasonal and climatic changes to the environment in which they live. Seasonal changes include variations in the duration of sunlight, precipitation, temperature, and other life-controlling factors. Studying the natural ways of plants gives one a nice springboard into learning more about ethnobotany. See "Internet Resources" for links to phenology networks.

Third, cultivate an ethical awareness of and respect for plants. Walk carefully on the earth. Don't take what you don't need, and never collect endangered plants or harvest in a way that damages a site. Stay current with plants' roles in the modern world. How can sustainable harvest be weighed against a growing need for raw resources? What is the effect of genetically modified plants on a plant-based worldview?

Enjoy your explorations!

Resources

Bremness, Lesley. *Herbs*. London: Dorling Kindersley, 1994.

Couplan, François, and James Duke. *The Encyclopedia of Edible Plants of North America*. New York: McGraw-Hill, 1998.

Foster, Steven, and Christopher Hobbs. *Western Medicinal Plants and Herbs*. Boston: Houghton/Mifflin, 2002.

Moerman, Daniel E. *Native American Medicinal Plants. An Ethnobotanical Dictionary*. Portland, OR: Timber Press, 2009.

Ody, Penelope. *The Complete Medicinal Herbal*. New York: DK, 1993.

Pojar, Jim, and Andy McKinnon. *Plants of the Pacific Northwest Coast: Washington, Oregon, British Columbia, and Alaska.* Redmond, WA: Lone Pine, 1994.

Stewart, Hilary. *Cedar.* Seattle: University of Washington Press, 1984.

Internet Resources

Earle, Christopher J. "The Gymnosperm Database." www.conifers.org/cu/th/plicata.htm.

"Nature's Calendar." (UK Phenology Network) www.naturescalendar.org.uk.

Pesznecker, Susan. "Salmon Feast Celebrates Fishing Heritage." 15 April 2006. Article available at www.ecotrust.org /news/psu_vanguard_0419.html.

"USA National Phenology Network." www.usanpn.org.

The Doctrine of Signatures

⤞ by J. Lee Lehman, PhD ⤝

D octrine of signatures? If you don't know what it is, it sounds strange, and not at all as if it has anything to do with plants. Church dogma? Handwriting analysis? The doctrine of signatures is an idea that germinated in many cultures which says that the medicinal properties of a plant (or sometimes animal or mineral) can be discerned from the appearance of the plant in question. So the liverwort was named such because its liver-like shape suggests that it would be useful for liver affectations, or conditions. In English, the suffix -wort denoted that the plant was thought to be useful for the condition indicated, so motherwort would

be useful for conditions related to pregnancy or childbirth. In the Mediterranean area, yet one more twist arose: these same properties were sometimes correlated with astrological ruler-ships. So an herb of Mars might be thought to have a sharp (acid) taste.

The doctrine of signatures is appealing for both practical and philosophical reasons. This idea fits in with belief in be-nefic spirits or gods who help humans to find medicines that will heal them. It provides confidence that it will be possible to find an appropriate remedy for a condition. It gives us the comforting sensation that the world is an orderly and rational place that can be comprehended.

This theory has been invented and reinvented time and again in the quest to see the living world and its relationship to human beings. It appears to be both a very old and a very common idea among different cultures. From an archeologi-cal perspective, we know that most cultures' creation myths attempt to explain how we came to be. In these myths, it was the gods who created us who had the power. Gods knew a lot more than we do, and while they might be capricious, they were seldom stupid. What would be the point, for example, of creating a creature without also creating food for the creature to eat? Why go to the trouble? Humans might be mandated to work to produce food, but there had to be a food source.

In a similar vein, it was difficult to see creation as com-pletely arbitrary. In a random world, plants might or might not have medicinal properties, and if they did, it would be impossible to tell what plant might be good for what condi-tion without extensive testing every step of the way. The pos-sibilities seem endless: hundreds of medical conditions and hundreds of plants, any of which could be entirely "useless." There might never be cures for anything!

But in the ordered world of the doctrine of signatures, how did people find out the uses of plants? There undoubtedly were shamanistic techniques that gave hints, but this is not a legacy that we can trace historically. What we do know is that, in Hellenistic culture by the time of Pliny the Elder (23–79 CE) and Dioscorides (fl. 50–70 CE), physicians and others had developed classification schemes for plants based on properties such as appearance and taste. There are analogous classification schemes for herbs in China and elsewhere. These methods provided a foundation for how a person could discover the medicinal properties of a new herb, based on knowledge about existing ones. These properties can be the basis for understanding plant use: if one plant has astringent properties, then another plant that has similar astringent properties would be expected to operate in a similar fashion.

But now, consider: does purple cone-flower (*Echinacea spp.*) look like yarrow (*Achillea millefolium*)? Both are woundworts. Does absinthe (*Artemisia absinthium*) look like valerian (*Valeriana officinalis*)? Both are emmenagogues—and also soporifics. One could argue in the case of woundworts that there were a lot of subtypes, such as woundworts for green wounds. But still: if you begin with the properties of plants, and then compare all the plants that have been designated as having that property, then you realize that if plants with similar medical properties do not look alike, then the doctrine of signatures is not actually used as much as practitioners think.

When a plant was said to be like something else, as in the doctrine of signatures, exactly what parts of the plant were used in this form of analogy? Today, botanical classification has been within the camp of Linnaeus (1707–1778) for centuries, and the portion of the plant that Linnaeus used as the primary system for classification was the flowering parts. In our days of cell biology and gene sequencing, there have been some modifications of systemics based on these more powerful tools, but mostly, these older systems of classification are still being used. However, prior to Linnaeus, as Stannard points out, Europeans tended to use leaf anatomy to classify plants.[1] This system results in different plants being seen as more similar to each other than we would currently aver. We can see this idea embedded in many old common names for plants, such as cinquefoil (literally five-leaved, known today as *Potentilla reptans*)—a name that dated back even to Middle English as pentafilon.

And yet, many names do not reflect the appearance of the plant, but its medical usage instead. Let's re-examine motherwort (*Leonurus cardiaca*), for instance. Motherwort was used in childbirth, but also for a condition that used to be called suffocation of the matrix: what we would now call hysteria. In our modern nomenclature, it's a nervine—so the older attribution to that somewhat suspect suffocation label is proved true. And it is still used for certain uterine and pregnancy issues. But its appearance? It's a perennial member of the mint family, with the signature square stem, and opposite leaf pattern with serrated leaves. There's not much there resembling a uterus!

Or take our friend yarrow, also known as soldier's woundwort. Its Latin name *Achillea millefolium* encapsulates its ap-

---

1. Stannard, Jerry. "A Fifteenth-Century Botanical Glossary." *Isis* 55.3 (1964): 358.

pearance: thousand-leaved, for the many tiny leaves. It contains salicyclic acid, the active ingredient in the wonder drug aspirin. There's little about its appearance that could be said to suggest its use, although I suppose somebody could say that the many leaves could represent an army.

And here we come to the main issue: is the doctrine of signatures a rigorously applied system for discovering the medicinal use of a plant, or either possibly a metaphor or a statement about one's belief in how the world works? I would argue the latter.

Perhaps the greatest statement of all time about the doctrine of signatures was that by the eighteenth century mystic Jacob Boehme, who began his work *Signatura Rerum* thus:

> All whatever is spoken, written, or taught of God, without the Knowledge of the Signature is dumb and void of Understanding; for it proceeds only from an historical Conjecture, from the mouth of another, wherein the Spirit without Knowledge is dumb; but if the Spirit opens to him the Signature, then he understand the Speech of another; and further he understands how the Spirit has manifested and revealed itself (out of the Essence through the Principle) in the Sound of the Voice."[2]

For our purposes, Boehme's use of "signature" can best be understood through its relationship to the word "sign." The concept of sign in the ancient world is very complex and sophisticated: we see examples in the Bible, and in such expressions as "signs of rain." In a world much closer to nature, people needed advance forecasts as much as we do. Lacking

---

2. Boehme, Jacob. *The Works of Jacob Behmen*. London, 1764, Volume IV, p 15. Available online at www.scribd.com/doc/395534/Jacob-Bohme-Vol-4-I-Signatura-Rerum.

satellites, they looked for ways to tell whether this growing season would be wet or dry, and they called these ways signs. They also used the same word for any communication with the gods. The doctrine of signatures could be reworded as "the doctrine of signs."

It is hard for us in our secular age to even begin to contemplate how enmeshed our ancestors were in worldviews where humans felt embedded in the great story of the universe that God or Gods created. We have lost the sense of creaturehood which this engendered—the experience of being created. In the absence of a higher power or powers, our story is the main attraction—not merely an unfolding of a piece of the Higher Plan. We have also lost our ability to relate to other species – and it is here that the doctrine of signatures belongs.

In a world with a benevolent Creator, or even a Creator who sees humans as overseers on Earth, signs are provided so that humans will know what to do. In Matthew 16:2–3, it says, "When it is evening, ye say, It will be fair weather: for the heaven is red. And in the morning, It will be foul weather to-day: for the heaven is red and lowering."[3] Signs are what separate us from a random universe. A mystic like Boehme sees signs everywhere, because these signs tell him that God is everywhere. One rendering of this idea in the West has been: as above, so below. But then, if this is true, then why don't all woundworts look alike, and why don't they all look like something related to wounds?

---

3. Matthew 16:2–3 from American Standard Version, www.earlychristianwritings.com/text/matthew-asv.html. This is the original wording of our English version, "red sky at night, sailor's delight ..."

To answer this question, we can begin by noting that within Western culture, one of the oldest forms of sign classification is celestial—astrology, by our parlance. Whether Babylonian or Egyptian, whether constellational or planetary, whether for weather forecasting or for mundane forecasting, the sky was easily seen as the canvas of the gods. One of the foremost historians of the field, Francesca Rochberg, titled her latest book on the subject *The Heavenly Writing*[4]— and this expression encapsulates the traditional understanding of the process. The realm of the gods was heaven, so anything seen in the heavens was necessarily of the gods or from the gods.

As the Babylonian understanding of the sky permeated other cultures, it mutated in its new environments, and took on new meanings and functions. Within the culture of Alexandria and elsewhere during Hellenistic times, a potent mix of philosophy, religion, medicine, and natural history produced such fruits as Neoplatonism, gnosticism, and Hellenistic astrology, which already had acquired a series of plant and other rulerships. Galen classified particular remedies by degree quality, as in hot and dry in the third degree. And during the same time period, we see the development of medicinal qualities of plants from Pliny and Dioscorides. Are these factors related?

Over twenty years ago, I became interested in this question: were the astrological rulerships of the plants given for their physical appearance or for their medical properties?

---

4. Rochberg, Francesca. *The Heavenly Writing: Divination, Horoscopy, and Astronomy in Mesopotamian Culture*. New York: Cambridge University Press, 2004.

When I took the plants given in Nicholas Culpeper's *Herbal* and classified them, it became clear that Culpeper's attributions of rulership were for medical reasons, not physical appearance.[5] What does this say about the doctrine of signatures?

Was the "signature" in question always a medical signature, not one based on physical appearance? Or perhaps the "signature" gradually changed from physical appearance to medical usage, and nobody really noticed the slip? If, as we have already observed, all plants with similar properties don't look exactly alike, then it's simply impossible for the doctrine of signatures to both describe appearance and function.

My own observations cannot really distinguish between these two possibilities, but intriguing research done since has approached the question from a different perspective. In an ethnological approach, Bennett studied the doctrine of signatures in a number of cultures and concluded that there actually is no evidence to suggest that it was ever used to classify plants, but that it still did have a very valuable function as a mnemonic device.[6] In other words, the appearance of a plant was not being used to decide upon its use, but, knowing its use, the appearance of the plant could be used to help to remember this information.

One other possibly important finding by Bennett identified the prevalence of strong-tasting or strong-odored plants

---

5. Lehman, J. Lee. *Essential Dignities*. Atglen, PA: Schiffer Press, 1989, 67–93.

6. Bennett, Bradley C. "Doctrine of Signatures: An Explanation of Medicinal Plant Discovery or Dissemination of Knowledge?" *Economic Botany* 61.3 (2007): 246–255.

in the pharmacopoeias. This is also fascinating, because it points out how herbalists over the centuries have used smell and taste to identify plants—and clearly, plant properties. Astringency is a good example of this—a medicinal property that is useful, especially for skin problems that need toning, or conditions relating to the old term "binding." Astringency is often a result of tannins, which are extremely sharp tasting. Thus, taste is actually a good diagnostic of property—in this case, much more so than the physical appearance of the plant. Having worked out its medicinal classification, it's now easy find something about the plant's physical appearance to remind you of its medical properties!

The human mind appears to constantly create relationships in order to understand its environment. As Aristotle said: "But the greatest thing by far is to have a command of metaphor. This alone cannot be imparted by another; it is the mark of genius, for to make good metaphors implies an eye for resemblances." (1459a4)[7]

Language is impossible without relating concept to word. Classification schemes are really just systems of relationships. And once we create these relationships, we may not even be sure how they happened. It appears that the basis for the doctrine of signatures was actually the creation of classification systems of plant medications for different diseases. These relationships—sometimes expressed astrologically, sometimes not—allowed herbalists and other practitioners to classify various plants under the same categories. Then, it appears,

---

7. The number is the Bekker number. The translation was: Aristotle, W. D. Ross, and J. A. Smith. *The Works of Aristotle*. Oxford: Clarendon Press, 1908.

these systems were "stored" by creating a relationship in the practitioner's mind between use and appearance. This process has been documented in non-literate societies, which developed different methods to remember. Many of these methods are at least as effective as pen on paper, although not so ideal for archaeologists!

It may at first seem that my own study and Bennett's refute the doctrine of signatures. They don't. What they addressed was what the actual use of the correspondences was for, not whether it was done, or even whether it was "true." The survival value of any mapping such as the doctrine of signatures was to help people get to a correct herb to help their condition—not necessarily *the* correct herb, but *a* correct herb. In order to do that, people either had to memorize long lists of what each herb was good for—and hope that the herb in question was available locally, and in flower, or otherwise in season for harvesting; or that somebody close by had had the foresight to gather it in the proper time and dry or otherwise preserve it. If none of this was the case, then you needed Plan B—or maybe even Plan F. Anything that allowed people to remember more woundworts or emmenagogues or diuretics had significant survival value. Different societies established different categories of medicinal classification, and then found physical indicators such as smell or taste—not to mention experimentation—to map different plants into these categories. It was the categories which were of such importance. The doctrine of signatures simply mapped the medicinal properties first, and appearance second.

The Future of Herbs

☙ by Diana Rajchel ❧

Herbs, those little green sub-versives poking their heads above ground just as we think they're gone, are plotting a revolution in photosynthetic collusion, appointing their gardeners as generals. Their battle strategies consist of guerilla actions: they have infiltrated foods and gardens, even our sidewalk cracks. They grow cells in our lawns, waiting and watching. We have had agents concealed in our spice racks for years, subtly enhancing the flavors of our lives. We are surrounded. They're ready to make their move, having signaled to our governments and medical agencies that they have power.

Herbs have more attention than they've ever garnered before, changing our world and oxygenating our lives. As antibiotics continue to fail, as we reclaim contaminated properties for public use and as we recognize how very much we need to find ways to generate oxygen to preserve a breathable atmosphere, herbs are creeping back in small armies with their sights set on the ecosphere. Watch out for those herbs—once they invade, they put down roots! Already, these little green men are repairing here, correcting there and through their hearty nature even overcoming some of the worst of the damage that we've done to the planet and to ourselves.

It looks to be a winning campaign for the chlorophyll set. The future of herbs glows green and vibrant with fresh approaches to old problems. Skyscraper rooftops will be dotted with herb gardens as cities offer greenroofing tax-break initiatives to reduce air pollution. Corporate farms will plant marigolds, garlic, and thyme between rows of major crops, having finally determined that the whole plant and not just an extraction keeps off parasites. Indoor and outdoor gardens will be absolutely commonplace, with all sorts of technical gadgetry to make their care easy and convenient. A media blitz about the healthful effects of indoor plants on people will create a boom in indoor gardening. This mushroom-shaped cloud looks like kombucha, as more individuals learn the benefits of cleansing tonics. Organic gardening will transition from "trend" to "norm" as most consumers expect and demand safe and flavorful food to eat. The advent of growing food locally, even within urban territories, will force even corporate farmers to revise their practices because if consumers feel dissatisfied by their food, they will return to the basics of raising their own.

The medical field will have the most complex advances. Nurse practitioners will lead the way in introducing live plants to hospital rooms, and greenhouse therapy as a post-treatment follow-up will begin with cancer patients but eventually become a routine practice after any surgical procedure. This therapy will involve simply bringing the patient into a greenhouse space attached to the hospital and letting that person enjoy the benefits of immediate, truly fresh air. These greenhouses will double as medical facilities, allowing on-site pharmacists to grow the plants needed for treatments. Since doctors are already overwhelmed with medical advancements, the role of the pharmacist will expand to include herbalism, and this will become a new specialization, as more pharmacists will need to be on hand who understand traditional medicine and how traditional drugs will interact with herbs.

The closed air of the urban space will see the most change. The once dry domain of African violets and spider plants will instead boast homegrown herbs and greens, thanks to affordable plant lights and easy installation. These urban herbs will arrive with a cultivated approach, insinuating themselves into continuously smaller spaces, even squatting on public land as guerilla gardeners use that perfectly good unattended public real estate. As we remember the enriching power of herbs, we will elevate their place in our lives. Rather than poisoning away our dandelions, we will know to harvest their greens. When an unfamiliar flower pops up among our petunias, we will look it up to determine what it is and how to use it. The future has roots, and the vines of change are creeping their way into our lives with health benefits and the ultimate artillery: good scent and great taste.

Herbs will storm our lives, freshen our minds, and gently guide us into a revolution where we can breathe easier, think more clearly, and enjoy the taste of simple living. They won't just be for farmers or homeowners—they will be uniquely urban, and city dwellers who love city dwelling will learn to look at their sidewalk cracks with a sense of possibility, build up their window boxes, and take pride in their food.

Herbs are already everywhere. They're already uniformed in green, biding their time in fertilizer-filled foxholes, waiting for their chance to take over. All it will take is a few more empirical studies, a few more gardens in neglected urban space, and a few more companies recognizing the cost-saving benefits of putting down a few plants. *Viva la revolución!*

Moon Signs, Phases, and Tables

The Quarters & Signs
of the Moon

Everyone has seen the Moon wax and wane through a period of approximately twenty-nine-and-a-half days. This circuit from New Moon to Full Moon and back again is called the lunation cycle. The cycle is divided into parts called quarters or phases. There are several methods by which this can be done, and the system used in the *Herbal Almanac* may not correspond to those used in other almanacs.

The Quarters
First Quarter

The First Quarter begins at the New Moon, when the Sun and Moon are in the same place, or conjunct. (This means that the Sun and Moon are in the same degree of the same sign.) The Moon is not visible at first, since it rises at the same time as the Sun. The New Moon is the time of new beginnings of projects that favor growth, externalization of activities, and the growth of ideas. The First Quarter is the time of germination, emergence, beginnings, and outwardly directed activity.

Second Quarter

The Second Quarter begins halfway between the new Moon and the full Moon, when the Sun and Moon are at right angles, or a ninety-degree square, to each other. This half Moon rises around noon and sets around midnight, so it can be seen in the western sky during the first half of the night. The Second Quarter is the time of growth and articulation of things that already exist.

Third Quarter

The Third Quarter begins at the Full Moon, when the Sun and Moon are opposite one another and the full light of the Sun can shine on the full sphere of the Moon. The round Moon can be seen rising in the east at sunset, and then rising a little later each evening. The Full Moon stands for illumination, fulfillment, culmination, completion, drawing inward, unrest, emotional expressions, and hasty actions leading to failure. The Third Quarter is a time of maturity, fruition, and the assumption of the full form of expression.

Fourth Quarter

The Fourth Quarter begins about halfway between the Full Moon and New Moon, when the Sun and Moon are again at ninety degrees, or square. This decreasing Moon rises at midnight and can be seen in the east during the last half of the night, reaching the overhead position just about as the sun rises. The Fourth Quarter is a time of disintegration and drawing back for reorganization and reflection.

The Signs
Moon in Aries

Moon in Aries is good for starting things, but lacking in staying power. Things occur rapidly, but also quickly pass.

Moon in Taurus

With Moon in Taurus, things begun during this sign last the longest and tend to increase in value. Things begun now become habitual and hard to alter.

Moon in Gemini

Moon in Gemini is an inconsistent position for the Moon, characterized by a lot of talk. Things begun now are easily changed by outside influences.

Moon in Cancer

Moon in Cancer stimulates emotional rapport between people. It pinpoints need and supports growth and nurturance.

Moon in Leo

Moon in Leo accents showmanship, being seen, drama, recreation, and happy pursuits. It may be concerned with praise and subject to flattery.

Moon in Virgo

Moon in Virgo favors accomplishment of details and commands from higher up, while discouraging independent thinking.

Moon in Libra

Moon in Libra increases self-awareness. This Moon favors self-examination and interaction with others, but discourages spontaneous initiative.

Moon in Scorpio

Moon in Scorpio increases awareness of psychic power. It precipitates psychic crises and ends connections thoroughly.

Moon in Sagittarius

Moon in Sagittarius encourages expansionary flights of imagination and confidence in the flow of life.

Moon in Capricorn

Moon in Capricorn increases awareness of the need for structure, discipline, and organization. Institutional activities are favored.

Moon in Aquarius

Moon in Aquarius favors activities that are unique and individualistic, concern for humanitarian needs and society as a whole, and improvements that can be made.

Moon in Pisces

During Moon in Pisces, energy withdraws from the surface of life and hibernates within, secretly reorganizing and realigning.

January Moon Table

Date	Sign	Element	Nature	Phase
1 Sun	Aries	Fire	Barren	2nd 1:15 am
2 Mon 5:16 pm	Taurus	Earth	Semi-fruitful	2nd
3 Tue	Taurus	Earth	Semi-fruitful	2nd
4 Wed	Taurus	Earth	Semi-fruitful	2nd
5 Thu 5:44 am	Gemini	Air	Barren	2nd
6 Fri	Gemini	Air	Barren	2nd
7 Sat 4:05 pm	Cancer	Water	Fruitful	2nd
8 Sun	Cancer	Water	Fruitful	2nd
9 Mon 11:35 pm	Leo	Fire	Barren	Full 2:30 am
10 Tue	Leo	Fire	Barren	3rd
11 Wed	Leo	Fire	Barren	3rd
12 Thu 4:44 am	Virgo	Earth	Barren	3rd
13 Fri	Virgo	Earth	Barren	3rd
14 Sat 8:28 am	Libra	Air	Semi-fruitful	3rd
15 Sun	Libra	Air	Semi-fruitful	3rd
16 Mon 11:33 am	Scorpio	Water	Fruitful	4th 4:08 am
17 Tue	Scorpio	Water	Fruitful	4th
18 Wed 2:29 pm	Sagittarius	Fire	Barren	4th
19 Thu	Sagittarius	Fire	Barren	4th
20 Fri 5:40 pm	Capricorn	Earth	Semi-fruitful	4th
21 Sat	Capricorn	Earth	Semi-fruitful	4th
22 Sun 9:53 pm	Aquarius	Air	Barren	4th
23 Mon	Aquarius	Air	Barren	New 2:39 am
24 Tue	Aquarius	Air	Barren	1st
25 Wed 4:11 am	Pisces	Water	Fruitful	1st
26 Thu	Pisces	Water	Fruitful	1st
27 Fri 1:28 pm	Aries	Fire	Barren	1st
28 Sat	Aries	Fire	Barren	1st
29 Sun	Aries	Fire	Barren	1st
30 Mon 1:28 am	Taurus	Earth	Semi-fruitful	2nd 11:10 pm
31 Tue	Taurus	Earth	Semi-fruitful	2nd

February Moon Table

Date	Sign	Element	Nature	Phase
1 Wed 2:14 pm	Gemini	Air	Barren	2nd
2 Thu	Gemini	Air	Barren	2nd
3 Fri	Gemini	Air	Barren	2nd
4 Sat 1:04 am	Cancer	Water	Fruitful	2nd
5 Sun	Cancer	Water	Fruitful	2nd
6 Mon 8:24 am	Leo	Fire	Barren	2nd
7 Tue	Leo	Fire	Barren	Full 4:54 pm
8 Wed 12:32 pm	Virgo	Earth	Barren	3rd
9 Thu	Virgo	Earth	Barren	3rd
10 Fri 2:54 pm	Libra	Air	Semi-fruitful	3rd
11 Sat	Libra	Air	Semi-fruitful	3rd
12 Sun 5:01 pm	Scorpio	Water	Fruitful	3rd
13 Mon	Scorpio	Water	Fruitful	3rd
14 Tue 7:56 pm	Sagittarius	Fire	Barren	4th 12:04 pm
15 Wed	Sagittarius	Fire	Barren	4th
16 Thu	Sagittarius	Fire	Barren	4th
17 Fri 12:03 am	Capricorn	Earth	Semi-fruitful	4th
18 Sat	Capricorn	Earth	Semi-fruitful	4th
19 Sun 5:28 am	Aquarius	Air	Barren	4th
20 Mon	Aquarius	Air	Barren	4th
21 Tue 12:31 pm	Pisces	Water	Fruitful	New 5:35 pm
22 Wed	Pisces	Water	Fruitful	1st
23 Thu 9:48 pm	Aries	Fire	Barren	1st
24 Fri	Aries	Fire	Barren	1st
25 Sat	Aries	Fire	Barren	1st
26 Sun 9:29 am	Taurus	Earth	Semi-fruitful	1st
27 Mon	Taurus	Earth	Semi-fruitful	1st
28 Tue 10:27 pm	Gemini	Air	Barren	1st
29 Wed	Gemini	Air	Barren	2nd 8:21 pm

March Moon Table

Date	Sign	Element	Nature	Phase
1 Thu	Gemini	Air	Barren	2nd
2 Fri 10:08 am	Cancer	Water	Fruitful	2nd
3 Sat	Cancer	Water	Fruitful	2nd
4 Sun 6:17 pm	Leo	Fire	Barren	2nd
5 Mon	Leo	Fire	Barren	2nd
6 Tue 10:27 pm	Virgo	Earth	Barren	2nd
7 Wed	Virgo	Earth	Barren	2nd
8 Thu 11:50 pm	Libra	Air	Semi-fruitful	Full 4:39 am
9 Fri	Libra	Air	Semi-fruitful	3rd
10 Sat	Libra	Air	Semi-fruitful	3rd
11 Sun 12:24 am	Scorpio	Water	Fruitful	3rd
12 Mon	Scorpio	Water	Fruitful	3rd
13 Tue 2:54 am	Sagittarius	Fire	Barren	3rd
14 Wed	Sagittarius	Fire	Barren	4th 9:25 pm
15 Thu 6:24 am	Capricorn	Earth	Semi-fruitful	4th
16 Fri	Capricorn	Earth	Semi-fruitful	4th
17 Sat 12:11 pm	Aquarius	Air	Barren	4th
18 Sun	Aquarius	Air	Barren	4th
19 Mon 8:05 pm	Pisces	Water	Fruitful	4th
20 Tue	Pisces	Water	Fruitful	4th
21 Wed	Pisces	Water	Fruitful	4th
22 Thu 5:57 am	Aries	Fire	Barren	New 10:37 am
23 Fri	Aries	Fire	Barren	1st
24 Sat 5:43 pm	Taurus	Earth	Semi-fruitful	1st
25 Sun	Taurus	Earth	Semi-fruitful	1st
26 Mon	Taurus	Earth	Semi-fruitful	1st
27 Tue 6:43 am	Gemini	Air	Barren	1st
28 Wed	Gemini	Air	Barren	1st
29 Thu 7:07 pm	Cancer	Water	Fruitful	1st
30 Fri	Cancer	Water	Fruitful	2nd 3:41 pm
31 Sat	Cancer	Water	Fruitful	2nd

April Moon Table

Date	Sign	Element	Nature	Phase
1 Sun 4:35 am	Leo	Fire	Barren	2nd
2 Mon	Leo	Fire	Barren	2nd
3 Tue 9:53 am	Virgo	Earth	Barren	2nd
4 Wed	Virgo	Earth	Barren	2nd
5 Thu 11:32 am	Libra	Air	Semi-fruitful	2nd
6 Fri	Libra	Air	Semi-fruitful	Full 3:19 pm
7 Sat 11:18 am	Scorpio	Water	Fruitful	3rd
8 Sun	Scorpio	Water	Fruitful	3rd
9 Mon 11:12 am	Sagittarius	Fire	Barren	3rd
10 Tue	Sagittarius	Fire	Barren	3rd
11 Wed 1:02 pm	Capricorn	Earth	Semi-fruitful	3rd
12 Thu	Capricorn	Earth	Semi-fruitful	3rd
13 Fri 5:48 pm	Aquarius	Air	Barren	4th 6:50 am
14 Sat	Aquarius	Air	Barren	4th
15 Sun	Aquarius	Air	Barren	4th
16 Mon 1:38 am	Pisces	Water	Fruitful	4th
17 Tue	Pisces	Water	Fruitful	4th
18 Wed 11:59 am	Aries	Fire	Barren	4th
19 Thu	Aries	Fire	Barren	4th
20 Fri	Aries	Fire	Barren	4th
21 Sat 12:05 am	Taurus	Earth	Semi-fruitful	New 3:18 am
22 Sun	Taurus	Earth	Semi-fruitful	1st
23 Mon 1:05 pm	Gemini	Air	Barren	1st
24 Tue	Gemini	Air	Barren	1st
25 Wed	Gemini	Air	Barren	1st
26 Thu 1:42 am	Cancer	Water	Fruitful	1st
27 Fri	Cancer	Water	Fruitful	1st
28 Sat 12:10 pm	Leo	Fire	Barren	1st
29 Sun	Leo	Fire	Barren	2nd 5:57 am
30 Mon 7:02 pm	Virgo	Earth	Barren	2nd

May Moon Table

Date	Sign	Element	Nature	Phase
1 Tue	Virgo	Earth	Barren	2nd
2 Wed 10:04 pm	Libra	Air	Semi-fruitful	2nd
3 Thu	Libra	Air	Semi-fruitful	2nd
4 Fri 10:20 pm	Scorpio	Water	Fruitful	2nd
5 Sat	Scorpio	Water	Fruitful	Full 11:35 pm
6 Sun 9:39 pm	Sagittarius	Fire	Barren	3rd
7 Mon	Sagittarius	Fire	Barren	3rd
8 Tue 10:00 pm	Capricorn	Earth	Semi-fruitful	3rd
9 Wed	Capricorn	Earth	Semi-fruitful	3rd
10 Thu	Capricorn	Earth	Semi-fruitful	3rd
11 Fri 1:03 am	Aquarius	Air	Barren	3rd
12 Sat	Aquarius	Air	Barren	4th 5:47 pm
13 Sun 7:42 am	Pisces	Water	Fruitful	4th
14 Mon	Pisces	Water	Fruitful	4th
15 Tue 5:45 pm	Aries	Fire	Barren	4th
16 Wed	Aries	Fire	Barren	4th
17 Thu	Aries	Fire	Barren	4th
18 Fri 6:03 am	Taurus	Earth	Semi-fruitful	4th
19 Sat	Taurus	Earth	Semi-fruitful	4th
20 Sun 7:05 pm	Gemini	Air	Barren	New 7:47 pm
21 Mon	Gemini	Air	Barren	1st
22 Tue	Gemini	Air	Barren	1st
23 Wed 7:31 am	Cancer	Water	Fruitful	1st
24 Thu	Cancer	Water	Fruitful	1st
25 Fri 6:11 pm	Leo	Fire	Barren	1st
26 Sat	Leo	Fire	Barren	1st
27 Sun	Leo	Fire	Barren	1st
28 Mon 2:06 am	Virgo	Earth	Barren	2nd 4:16 pm
29 Tue	Virgo	Earth	Barren	2nd
30 Wed 6:46 am	Libra	Air	Semi-fruitful	2nd
31 Thu	Libra	Air	Semi-fruitful	2nd

June Moon Table

Date	Sign	Element	Nature	Phase
1 Fri 8:31 am	Scorpio	Water	Fruitful	2nd
2 Sat	Scorpio	Water	Fruitful	2nd
3 Sun 8:32 am	Sagittarius	Fire	Barren	2nd
4 Mon	Sagittarius	Fire	Barren	Full 7:12 am
5 Tue 8:31 am	Capricorn	Earth	Semi-fruitful	3rd
6 Wed	Capricorn	Earth	Semi-fruitful	3rd
7 Thu 10:17 am	Aquarius	Air	Barren	3rd
8 Fri	Aquarius	Air	Barren	3rd
9 Sat 3:22 pm	Pisces	Water	Fruitful	3rd
10 Sun	Pisces	Water	Fruitful	3rd
11 Mon	Pisces	Water	Fruitful	4th 6:41 am
12 Tue 12:21 am	Aries	Fire	Barren	4th
13 Wed	Aries	Fire	Barren	4th
14 Thu 12:22 pm	Taurus	Earth	Semi-fruitful	4th
15 Fri	Taurus	Earth	Semi-fruitful	4th
16 Sat	Taurus	Earth	Semi-fruitful	4th
17 Sun 1:24 am	Gemini	Air	Barren	4th
18 Mon	Gemini	Air	Barren	4th
19 Tue 1:34 pm	Cancer	Water	Fruitful	New 11:02 am
20 Wed	Cancer	Water	Fruitful	1st
21 Thu 11:47 pm	Leo	Fire	Barren	1st
22 Fri	Leo	Fire	Barren	1st
23 Sat	Leo	Fire	Barren	1st
24 Sun 7:42 am	Virgo	Earth	Barren	1st
25 Mon	Virgo	Earth	Barren	1st
26 Tue 1:15 pm	Libra	Air	Semi-fruitful	2nd 11:30 pm
27 Wed	Libra	Air	Semi-fruitful	2nd
28 Thu 4:32 pm	Scorpio	Water	Fruitful	2nd
29 Fri	Scorpio	Water	Fruitful	2nd
30 Sat 6:04 pm	Sagittarius	Fire	Barren	2nd

July Moon Table

Date	Sign	Element	Nature	Phase
1 Sun	Sagittarius	Fire	Barren	2nd
2 Mon 6:51 pm	Capricorn	Earth	Semi-fruitful	2nd
3 Tue	Capricorn	Earth	Semi-fruitful	Full 2:52 pm
4 Wed 8:26 pm	Aquarius	Air	Barren	3rd
5 Thu	Aquarius	Air	Barren	3rd
6 Fri	Aquarius	Air	Barren	3rd
7 Sat 12:29 am	Pisces	Water	Fruitful	3rd
8 Sun	Pisces	Water	Fruitful	3rd
9 Mon 8:14 am	Aries	Fire	Barren	3rd
10 Tue	Aries	Fire	Barren	4th 9:48 pm
11 Wed 7:30 pm	Taurus	Earth	Semi-fruitful	4th
12 Thu	Taurus	Earth	Semi-fruitful	4th
13 Fri	Taurus	Earth	Semi-fruitful	4th
14 Sat 8:26 am	Gemini	Air	Barren	4th
15 Sun	Gemini	Air	Barren	4th
16 Mon 8:31 pm	Cancer	Water	Fruitful	4th
17 Tue	Cancer	Water	Fruitful	4th
18 Wed	Cancer	Water	Fruitful	4th
19 Thu 6:13 am	Leo	Fire	Barren	New 12:24 am
20 Fri	Leo	Fire	Barren	1st
21 Sat 1:24 pm	Virgo	Earth	Barren	1st
22 Sun	Virgo	Earth	Barren	1st
23 Mon 6:38 pm	Libra	Air	Semi-fruitful	1st
24 Tue	Libra	Air	Semi-fruitful	1st
25 Wed 10:29 pm	Scorpio	Water	Fruitful	1st
26 Thu	Scorpio	Water	Fruitful	2nd 4:56 am
27 Fri	Scorpio	Water	Fruitful	2nd
28 Sat 1:18 am	Sagittarius	Fire	Barren	2nd
29 Sun	Sagittarius	Fire	Barren	2nd
30 Mon 3:29 am	Capricorn	Earth	Semi-fruitful	2nd
31 Tue	Capricorn	Earth	Semi-fruitful	2nd

August Moon Table

Date	Sign	Element	Nature	Phase
1 Wed 5:56 am	Aquarius	Air	Barren	Full 11:27 pm
2 Thu	Aquarius	Air	Barren	3rd
3 Fri 9:58 am	Pisces	Water	Fruitful	3rd
4 Sat	Pisces	Water	Fruitful	3rd
5 Sun 4:59 pm	Aries	Fire	Barren	3rd
6 Mon	Aries	Fire	Barren	3rd
7 Tue	Aries	Fire	Barren	3rd
8 Wed 3:28 am	Taurus	Earth	Semi-fruitful	3rd
9 Thu	Taurus	Earth	Semi-fruitful	4th 2:55 pm
10 Fri 4:11 pm	Gemini	Air	Barren	4th
11 Sat	Gemini	Air	Barren	4th
12 Sun	Gemini	Air	Barren	4th
13 Mon 4:27 am	Cancer	Water	Fruitful	4th
14 Tue	Cancer	Water	Fruitful	4th
15 Wed 2:05 pm	Leo	Fire	Barren	4th
16 Thu	Leo	Fire	Barren	4th
17 Fri 8:33 pm	Virgo	Earth	Barren	New 11:54 am
18 Sat	Virgo	Earth	Barren	1st
19 Sun	Virgo	Earth	Barren	1st
20 Mon 12:45 am	Libra	Air	Semi-fruitful	1st
21 Tue	Libra	Air	Semi-fruitful	1st
22 Wed 3:54 am	Scorpio	Water	Fruitful	1st
23 Thu	Scorpio	Water	Fruitful	1st
24 Fri 6:50 am	Sagittarius	Fire	Barren	2nd 9:54 am
25 Sat	Sagittarius	Fire	Barren	2nd
26 Sun 9:58 am	Capricorn	Earth	Semi-fruitful	2nd
27 Mon	Capricorn	Earth	Semi-fruitful	2nd
28 Tue 1:38 pm	Aquarius	Air	Barren	2nd
29 Wed	Aquarius	Air	Barren	2nd
30 Thu 6:31 pm	Pisces	Water	Fruitful	2nd
31 Fri	Pisces	Water	Fruitful	Full 9:58 am

September Moon Table

Date	Sign	Element	Nature	Phase
1 Sat	Pisces	Water	Fruitful	3rd
2 Sun 1:37 am	Aries	Fire	Barren	3rd
3 Mon	Aries	Fire	Barren	3rd
4 Tue 11:41 am	Taurus	Earth	Semi-fruitful	3rd
5 Wed	Taurus	Earth	Semi-fruitful	3rd
6 Thu	Taurus	Earth	Semi-fruitful	3rd
7 Fri 12:10 am	Gemini	Air	Barren	3rd
8 Sat	Gemini	Air	Barren	4th 9:15 am
9 Sun 12:49 pm	Cancer	Water	Fruitful	4th
10 Mon	Cancer	Water	Fruitful	4th
11 Tue 11:00 pm	Leo	Fire	Barren	4th
12 Wed	Leo	Fire	Barren	4th
13 Thu	Leo	Fire	Barren	4th
14 Fri 5:30 am	Virgo	Earth	Barren	4th
15 Sat	Virgo	Earth	Barren	New 10:11 pm
16 Sun 8:55 am	Libra	Air	Semi-fruitful	1st
17 Mon	Libra	Air	Semi-fruitful	1st
18 Tue 10:46 am	Scorpio	Water	Fruitful	1st
19 Wed	Scorpio	Water	Fruitful	1st
20 Thu 12:34 pm	Sagittarius	Fire	Barren	1st
21 Fri	Sagittarius	Fire	Barren	1st
22 Sat 3:20 pm	Capricorn	Earth	Semi-fruitful	2nd 3:41 pm
23 Sun	Capricorn	Earth	Semi-fruitful	2nd
24 Mon 7:32 pm	Aquarius	Air	Barren	2nd
25 Tue	Aquarius	Air	Barren	2nd
26 Wed	Aquarius	Air	Barren	2nd
27 Thu 1:23 am	Pisces	Water	Fruitful	2nd
28 Fri	Pisces	Water	Fruitful	2nd
29 Sat 9:14 am	Aries	Fire	Barren	Full 11:19 pm
30 Sun	Aries	Fire	Barren	3rd

October Moon Table

Date	Sign	Element	Nature	Phase
1 Mon 7:26 pm	Taurus	Earth	Semi-fruitful	3rd
2 Tue	Taurus	Earth	Semi-fruitful	3rd
3 Wed	Taurus	Earth	Semi-fruitful	3rd
4 Thu 7:47 am	Gemini	Air	Barren	3rd
5 Fri	Gemini	Air	Barren	3rd
6 Sat 8:45 pm	Cancer	Water	Fruitful	3rd
7 Sun	Cancer	Water	Fruitful	3rd
8 Mon	Cancer	Water	Fruitful	4th 3:33 am
9 Tue 7:55 am	Leo	Fire	Barren	4th
10 Wed	Leo	Fire	Barren	4th
11 Thu 3:23 pm	Virgo	Earth	Barren	4th
12 Fri	Virgo	Earth	Barren	4th
13 Sat 7:02 pm	Libra	Air	Semi-fruitful	4th
14 Sun	Libra	Air	Semi-fruitful	4th
15 Mon 8:06 pm	Scorpio	Water	Fruitful	New 8:02 am
16 Tue	Scorpio	Water	Fruitful	1st
17 Wed 8:26 pm	Sagittarius	Fire	Barren	1st
18 Thu	Sagittarius	Fire	Barren	1st
19 Fri 9:41 pm	Capricorn	Earth	Semi-fruitful	1st
20 Sat	Capricorn	Earth	Semi-fruitful	1st
21 Sun	Capricorn	Earth	Semi-fruitful	2nd 11:32 pm
22 Mon 1:02 am	Aquarius	Air	Barren	2nd
23 Tue	Aquarius	Air	Barren	2nd
24 Wed 7:00 am	Pisces	Water	Fruitful	2nd
25 Thu	Pisces	Water	Fruitful	2nd
26 Fri 3:31 pm	Aries	Fire	Barren	2nd
27 Sat	Aries	Fire	Barren	2nd
28 Sun	Aries	Fire	Barren	2nd
29 Mon 2:15 am	Taurus	Earth	Semi-fruitful	Full 3:49 pm
30 Tue	Taurus	Earth	Semi-fruitful	3rd
31 Wed 2:40 pm	Gemini	Air	Barren	3rd

November Moon Table

Date	Sign	Element	Nature	Phase
1 Thu	Gemini	Air	Barren	3rd
2 Fri	Gemini	Air	Barren	3rd
3 Sat 3:43 am	Cancer	Water	Fruitful	3rd
4 Sun	Cancer	Water	Fruitful	3rd
5 Mon 2:39 pm	Leo	Fire	Barren	3rd
6 Tue	Leo	Fire	Barren	4th 7:36 pm
7 Wed 11:35 pm	Virgo	Earth	Barren	4th
8 Thu	Virgo	Earth	Barren	4th
9 Fri	Virgo	Earth	Barren	4th
10 Sat 4:35 am	Libra	Air	Semi-fruitful	4th
11 Sun	Libra	Air	Semi-fruitful	4th
12 Mon 6:10 am	Scorpio	Water	Fruitful	4th
13 Tue	Scorpio	Water	Fruitful	New 5:08 pm
14 Wed 5:52 am	Sagittarius	Fire	Barren	1st
15 Thu	Sagittarius	Fire	Barren	1st
16 Fri 5:35 am	Capricorn	Earth	Semi-fruitful	1st
17 Sat	Capricorn	Earth	Semi-fruitful	1st
18 Sun 7:10 am	Aquarius	Air	Barren	1st
19 Mon	Aquarius	Air	Barren	1st
20 Tue 11:55 am	Pisces	Water	Fruitful	2nd 9:31 am
21 Wed	Pisces	Water	Fruitful	2nd
22 Thu 8:12 pm	Aries	Fire	Barren	2nd
23 Fri	Aries	Fire	Barren	2nd
24 Sat	Aries	Fire	Barren	2nd
25 Sun 7:18 am	Taurus	Earth	Semi-fruitful	2nd
26 Mon	Taurus	Earth	Semi-fruitful	2nd
27 Tue 7:58 pm	Gemini	Air	Barren	2nd
28 Wed	Gemini	Air	Barren	Full 9:46 am
29 Thu	Gemini	Air	Barren	3rd
30 Fri 8:55 am	Cancer	Water	Fruitful	3rd

December Moon Table

Date	Sign	Element	Nature	Phase
1 Sat	Cancer	Water	Fruitful	3rd
2 Sun 8:57 pm	Leo	Fire	Barren	3rd
3 Mon	Leo	Fire	Barren	3rd
4 Tue	Leo	Fire	Barren	3rd
5 Wed 6:51 am	Virgo	Earth	Barren	3rd
6 Thu	Virgo	Earth	Barren	4th 10:31 am
7 Fri 1:35 pm	Libra	Air	Semi-fruitful	4th
8 Sat	Libra	Air	Semi-fruitful	4th
9 Sun 4:51 pm	Scorpio	Water	Fruitful	4th
10 Mon	Scorpio	Water	Fruitful	4th
11 Tue 5:22 pm	Sagittarius	Fire	Barren	4th
12 Wed	Sagittarius	Fire	Barren	4th
13 Thu 4:43 pm	Capricorn	Earth	Semi-fruitful	New 3:42 am
14 Fri	Capricorn	Earth	Semi-fruitful	1st
15 Sat 4:53 pm	Aquarius	Air	Barren	1st
16 Sun	Aquarius	Air	Barren	1st
17 Mon 7:48 pm	Pisces	Water	Fruitful	1st
18 Tue	Pisces	Water	Fruitful	1st
19 Wed	Pisces	Water	Fruitful	1st
20 Thu 2:43 am	Aries	Fire	Barren	2nd 12:19 am
21 Fri	Aries	Fire	Barren	2nd
22 Sat 1:25 pm	Taurus	Earth	Semi-fruitful	2nd
23 Sun	Taurus	Earth	Semi-fruitful	2nd
24 Mon	Taurus	Earth	Semi-fruitful	2nd
25 Tue 2:13 am	Gemini	Air	Barren	2nd
26 Wed	Gemini	Air	Barren	2nd
27 Thu 3:06 pm	Cancer	Water	Fruitful	2nd
28 Fri	Cancer	Water	Fruitful	Full 5:21 am
29 Sat	Cancer	Water	Fruitful	3rd
30 Sun 2:45 am	Leo	Fire	Barren	3rd
31 Mon	Leo	Fire	Barren	3rd

Dates to Destroy Weeds and Pests

From		To		Sign	Qtr.
Jan 9	11:35 pm	Jan 12	4:44 am	Leo	3rd
Jan 12	4:44 am	Jan 14	8:28 am	Virgo	3rd
Jan 18	2:29 pm	Jan 20	5:40 pm	Sagittarius	4th
Jan 22	9:53 pm	Jan 23	2:39 am	Aquarius	4th
Feb 7	4:54 pm	Feb 8	12:32 pm	Leo	3rd
Feb 8	12:32 pm	Feb 10	2:54 pm	Virgo	3rd
Feb 14	7:56 pm	Feb 17	12:03 am	Sagittarius	4th
Feb 19	5:28 am	Feb 21	12:31 pm	Aquarius	4th
Mar 8	4:39 am	Mar 8	11:50 pm	Virgo	3rd
Mar 13	2:54 am	Mar 14	9:25 pm	Sagittarius	3rd
Mar 14	9:25 pm	Mar 15	6:24 am	Sagittarius	4th
Mar 17	12:11 pm	Mar 19	8:05 pm	Aquarius	4th
Mar 22	5:57 am	Mar 22	10:37 am	Aries	4th
Apr 9	11:12 am	Apr 11	1:02 pm	Sagittarius	3rd
Apr 13	5:48 pm	Apr 16	1:38 am	Aquarius	4th
Apr 18	11:59 am	Apr 21	12:05 am	Aries	4th
May 6	9:39 pm	May 8	10:00 pm	Sagittarius	3rd
May 11	1:03 am	May 12	5:47 pm	Aquarius	3rd
May 12	5:47 pm	May 13	7:42 am	Aquarius	4th
May 15	5:45 pm	May 18	6:03 am	Aries	4th
May 20	7:05 pm	May 20	7:47 pm	Gemini	4th
Jun 4	7:12 am	Jun 5	8:31 am	Sagittarius	3rd
Jun 7	10:17 am	Jun 9	3:22 pm	Aquarius	3rd
Jun 12	12:21 am	Jun 14	12:22 pm	Aries	4th
Jun 17	1:24 am	Jun 19	11:02 am	Gemini	4th
Jul 4	8:26 pm	Jul 7	12:29 am	Aquarius	3rd

Jul 9	8:14 am	Jul 10	9:48 pm	Aries	3rd
Jul 10	9:48 pm	Jul 11	7:30 pm	Aries	4th
Jul 14	8:26 am	Jul 16	8:31 pm	Gemini	4th
Aug 1	11:27 pm	Aug 3	9:58 am	Aquarius	3rd
Aug 5	4:59 pm	Aug 8	3:28 am	Aries	3rd
Aug 10	4:11 pm	Aug 13	4:27 am	Gemini	4th
Aug 15	2:05 pm	Aug 17	11:54 am	Leo	4th
Sep 2	1:37 am	Sep 4	11:41 am	Aries	3rd
Sep 7	12:10 am	Sep 8	9:15 am	Gemini	3rd
Sep 8	9:15 am	Sep 9	12:49 pm	Gemini	4th
Sep 11	11:00 pm	Sep 14	5:30 am	Leo	4th
Sep 14	5:30 am	Sep 15	10:11 pm	Virgo	4th
Sep 29	11:19 pm	Oct 1	7:26 pm	Aries	3rd
Oct 4	7:47 am	Oct 6	8:45 pm	Gemini	3rd
Oct 9	7:55 am	Oct 11	3:23 pm	Leo	4th
Oct 11	3:23 pm	Oct 13	7:02 pm	Virgo	4th
Oct 31	2:40 pm	Nov 3	3:43 am	Gemini	3rd
Nov 5	2:39 pm	Nov 6	7:36 pm	Leo	3rd
Nov 6	7:36 pm	Nov 7	11:35 pm	Leo	4th
Nov 7	11:35 pm	Nov 10	4:35 am	Virgo	4th
Nov 28	9:46 am	Nov 30	8:55 am	Gemini	3rd
Dec 2	8:57 pm	Dec 5	6:51 am	Leo	3rd
Dec 5	6:51 am	Dec 6	10:31 am	Virgo	3rd
Dec 6	10:31 am	Dec 7	1:35 pm	Virgo	4th
Dec 11	5:22 pm	Dec 13	3:42 am	Sagittarius	4th
Dec 30	2:45 am	Jan 1, 2013	12:35 pm	Leo	3rd

About the Authors

ELIZABETH BARRETTE is a resident of central Illinois and has been involved with the Pagan community for more than seventeen years. Her other writing fields include speculative fiction and gender studies. To find out more about Elizabeth, visit her website at www.worthlink.net/~ysabet/sitemap.html.

CALANTIRNIEL has worked with herbs and natural healing since the early 1990s and became a certified master herbalist in 2007. She lives in western Montana with her husband and daughter while her son is off to college. She also manages to have an organic garden and crochets professionally. Find out more at www.myspace.com/aartiana.

DALLAS JENNIFER COBB loves family, gardens, fitness, and fabulous food. Contact her at Jennifer.Cobb@Sympatico.ca.

ALICE DEVILLE is an internationally known astrologer, writer, and metaphysical consultant. She has been both a reiki and seichim master since 1996. In her northern Virginia practice, Alice specializes in relationships, health, healing, real estate, government affairs, career and change management, and spiritual development. Contact Alice at DeVilleAA@aol.com.

SEAN DONAHUE is a traditional herbalist who works primarily with the wild plants of the forests and fields of New England. He views the plants as teachers, helping the body, mind, and spirit learn to correct imbalances that stand in the way of health. He lives in Maine, with his partner, Darcey Blue French, and their Siberian Husky, Trill. He blogs at http://greenmanramblings.blogspot.com.

DARCEY BLUE FRENCH trained as a clinical herbalist and nutritionist at the North American Institute of Medical Herbalism under Paul Bergner. It is her deep love of the wild Earth and its creatures that fuels her passion for healing and teaching about plants, wilderness, spirit, nourishment, and healing. You can learn more about her at www.brighidswellherbs.com.

JD Hortwort resides in North Carolina. She is an avid student of herbology and gardening, a professional writer, and an award-winning journalist.

Lucy Hall Kelly is a graduate of Eastern Kentucky University with bachelors degree in Social Work. Lucy is a freelance writer and lifelong enthusiast of folklore, mythology, and the occult. She currently resides in the foothills of the Appalachian mountains of southwest Virginia and works for a Virginia social services agency. She has written for *FATE* magazine and has articles in upcoming issues of *Doll Collector*.

Misty Kuceris has worked as a plant specialist for various nurseries in the Greater DC metropolitan area, and in 2011 she became a Virginia Certified Horticulturist. She consults and lectures on how to create healthy home gardens and lawns. You can contact her at Misty@EnhanceOneself.com with any questions.

J. Lee Lehman has a Ph.D. in Botany from Rutgers University. Lee is a partner in sheville.org, an online community magazine that features resources relating to the feminist ideals of balance, collaboration, compassion, and environmental stewardship that challenge greed, exploitation, and domination. You can find out more about Lee at http://leelehman .com/joomla15.

Sharynne MacLeod NicMhacha is a Celtic teacher, writer and bard of Scottish, Irish and Welshancestry, and a direct descendant of 'Fairy Clan' MacLeod. She trained in Celtic Studies through Harvard University, and has presented and published work in North America, Ireland, and Scotland. Sharynne serves as Faculty in Celtic Pagan religion and shamanism at Omega, Kripalu, and Rowe, and is also a Faculty Member of the Celtic Institute of North America.

Susan Pesznecker is a child of the natural world and a student of astronomy, herbology, healing, stonework, nature study, and folklore. Susan is an aficionado of the rock art of Northwest Coastal and Columbia Plateau First People. She loves to read, camp, and work in her organic garden at her home in Milwaukie, Oregon.

Linda Raedisch writes about folklore, religion, and holidays. Taking the term "garden apartments" at face value, she grows a variety of New World natives on and around her doorstep. She lives in Zone 7.

Diana Rajchel lives, works, worships, and writes in Minneapolis, Minnesota. Sometimes she works with organizations that need assistance in the care and feeding of volunteers. You can learn more about her at www.dianarajchel.com.

Suzanne Ress is an accomplished self-taught gardener and silversmith/mosiacist. She lives in the woods at the foot of the Alps in northern Italy with her husband, two teenage daughters, wolf dog, and two horses.

Janice Sharkey is an aromatherapist and astrological gardener. She loves scented plants and, most of all, herbs. When she's not gardening, she's making stained glass panels or writing. One of her ambitions is to get her children David and Rose and her husband William to spend more time in the garden.

Harmony Usher lives in Prince Edward County, Ontario, with her two children, a super dog, and a magical boy rabbit.

Tess Whitehurst is the author of *Magical Housekeeping: Simple Charms and Practical Tips for Creating a Harmonious Home* and *The Good Energy Book: Creating Harmony and Balance for Yourself and Your Home*.